W9-BXN-069

Warrior • 113

US Army Soldier

Baghdad 2003–04

Kenneth W Estes • Illustrated by Howard Gerrard

First published in Great Britain in 2007 by Osprey Publishing,
Midland House, West Way, Botley, Oxford OX2 0PH, UK
443 Park Avenue South, New York, NY 10016, USA
E-mail: info@ospreypublishing.com

A CIP catalog record for this book is available from the British Library

ISBN: 978 1 84603 063 5

Page layout by: Ken Vail Graphic Design, Cambridge, UK
Index by David Worthington
Typeset in Helvetica Neue and ITC New Baskerville
Originated by United Graphics Ltd, Singapore, UK
Printed in China through Worldprint

07 08 09 10 11   10 9 8 7 6 5 4 3 2 1

FOR A CATALOG OF ALL BOOKS PUBLISHED BY OSPREY MILITARY AND
AVIATION PLEASE CONTACT:

NORTH AMERICA
Osprey Direct, c/o Random House Distribution Center, 400 Hahn Road,
Westminster, MD 21157
E-mail: info@ospreydirect.com

ALL OTHER REGIONS
Osprey Direct UK, P.O. Box 140 Wellingborough, Northants, NN8 2FA, UK
E-mail: info@ospreydirect.co.uk

www.ospreypublishing.com

Artist's note

Readers may care to note that the original paintings from
which the color plates in this book were prepared are
available for private sale. All reproduction copyright
whatsoever is retained by the Publishers. All inquiries
should be addressed to:

Howard Gerrard
11 Oaks Road
Tenterden
Kent
TN30 6RD
UK

The Publishers regret that they can enter into no
correspondence upon this matter.

Dedication

To William H. Russell, professor of history and mentor, US
Naval Academy.

Acknowledgments

The author is indebted to many individuals. MG (now LTG)
Martin Dempsey first invited me to research and write the
command narrative of the campaign of Task Force (TF)
Baghdad, built around his 1st Armored Division command.
I benefited greatly from discussions in 2005 with him and
many of the officers and NCOs of the division who served
in the campaign, including BG Michael Tucker, Col George
Lockwood, Maj Thomas Crowson, Maj Laurence Brown,
Maj Steven Letcher, CSM Roger Blackwood, MSG David
Melancon, and SFC Darrin Goode. I also spent several hours
interviewing each of the following: Col Ralph Baker, Col Peter
Mansoor, Col Jonathan Brockman, Col Dyfierd Harris,
Col Louis Marich, Col Russell Gold, LTC Dale Ringler, and
Maj Eric Wick. Captains Tom Noble and Chris Kane were my
"handlers," and Mr. Steve Ruhnke, director of the 1st Armored
Division Museum, and Army historians at the Heidelberg office
– Dr. Charles E. Kirkpatrick (V Corps, who sadly died on
October 29, 2005) and Dr. Kevin McKedy (US Army, Europe –
USAREUR) – all provided invaluable assistance. Kenneth
Melendy, Andrew Dziengeleski, and Daniel Shepetis read early
versions of the manuscript and made cogent suggestions.

Photographs are official US Army unless otherwise noted.

Rank abbreviations

Note the following US Army rank abbreviations occur in
this book:

SGT	Sergeant
SSG	Staff Sergeant
CSM	Color Sergeant Major
Maj	Major
LTC	Lieutenant Colonel
Col	Colonel
BG	Brigadier General
MG	Major General
LTG	Lieutenant General
Gen	General

CONTENTS

US ARMY SOLDIER: BAGHDAD 2003–04

INTRODUCTION

On May 12, 2003, the 1st Battalion, 13th Armor (1/13th) convoyed to Baghdad, where it attached to the 3d Infantry Division for occupation duty. Even though the 1/13th's tanks and armored convoys entered the city after the US President's declaration that all "major combat operations" had ended, the tracers illuminating the night sky and rumbles of explosions in the distance gave a very different impression to the soldiers. The 1/13th Armor joined its parent 3d Brigade, 1st Armored Division (3d/1st) as the "Bulldog" brigade settled into its Baghdad zone as the first of the armored division's major units to initiate Phase IVB (post-hostility) operations there.

The deployment of the 1st Armored Division ("Old Ironsides") and its reinforcing units to the capital city of Iraq in 2003–04 contains many surprising turns of event. Originally slated for the opening invasion, the armored division instead became the senior organization responsible for Baghdad's occupation. Situations did not always appear well oriented and often it required the tenacious efforts, skills, courage, and stamina of "Iron Soldiers" and their comrades to reach the desired outcome. The combat record of Old Ironsides in Iraq brings great credit upon the US Army and the armed forces of the United States of America. It lies interspersed with a seemingly endless range of tasks undertaken by the division and the task force it led, as it engaged in security and stabilization operations in Baghdad and the surrounding provinces.

During a cordon and search operation, this staff sergeant (left) gestures to his section, off camera, to move to the flank. Remaining close by is his automatic rifleman, armed with the M249 Squad Automatic Weapon (SAW). Both men wear Interceptor vests with Small Arms Protective Inserts (SAPI), but other equipment varies. The helmet scope mount on the SAW-man is the screw-on type, and the SSG has an M-203 40mm grenade launcher, 4× scope and AN/PEQ-2 laser pointer attached to his M4 carbine, for which he also wears the 40mm ammunition vest. The All-purpose Lightweight Individual Carrying Equipment (ALICE)-type magazine and grenade pouches are attached directly to the Interceptor vests, instead of using web gear, thus minimizing bulk and possible snags. Both wear kneepads; the leader is also wearing a leg strap clipboard on his right thigh and a transceiver on a carabineer clip.

So scarce were the Up-Armored HMMWVs (UAHs) that soldiers naturally began to improvise add-on protection, often as simple as hanging bags containing Kevlar® plates salvaged from vests and vehicles on the exterior of the otherwise thinly covered Humvee doors.

"Nation building" has existed as a military mission for the US Army throughout its history. In contemporary usage, it has sent chills through the ranks of politicos, pundits, and observers, and not a few serving military leaders. Nevertheless, most of the activities of the division fell within the main descriptions of nation building in its classic sense. The restoration of order in the capital, humanitarian assistance, training of security forces, and the facilitating of local government initially formed the bedrock of US and coalition actions in Baghdad. In addition, the concerted efforts by Task Force (TF) 1st Armored Division to repair and reconstruct the city infrastructure far exceeded the war damage sustained in the US occupation of Iraq in March–April 2003. In reality, the US forces began a long process of helping the local people to recover from the lengthy deprivation suffered under Saddam Hussein's dictatorial regime.

The emerging evidence of the 2003–04 campaign by the TF 1st Armored Division and other elements of the US Central Command (USCENTCOM) will be debated by army institutions for decades to come. Few examples exist in US history of the extremes in operational employment experienced by the task force. War in Iraq was foreseen and planned for over a year by the division, which prepared for a decisive role in V Corps' planning for the attack and seizure of the country. Despite this preparation for sustained high-intensity combat, only elements of its 3d Brigade would participate in the initial campaign. The deployment of the division from its posts in Germany brought it to the gates of Baghdad just in time for it to take the reins of authority for a mission not yet clear.

The military occupation of Baghdad called for the utmost of patience, perseverance, and fortitude, among many other requirements. The city was damaged, its inhabitants demoralized, and little vestige of civil authority remained. Hopes remained high, however, that the occupation would prove limited or even unnecessary and that the Iraqis would pick themselves up and begin a rebuilding process in the light of newly gained freedom. But as the 1st Armored Division took up its new and unplanned responsibilities, various forms of insurgency began to emerge and present increasing security threats to its soldiers and the citizens. For the division, nation building and combat operations would proceed in tandem, if not simultaneously, for almost all of its service in Iraq.

The most extraordinary set of circumstances Old Ironsides experienced lay a year ahead. As the summer of 2004 approached, with the division's mission virtually accomplished and the turnover of its responsibilities for the city at hand, a new threat presented itself. A fresh uprising cut off land communications south of Kuwait, over which division units were even then convoying as the planned redeployment began. Baghdad and other cities erupted with new violence and armed insurrection came into the open as never before. Instead of returning to home posts, the 1st Armored Division and 2d Armored Cavalry Regiment (2d ACR) had to stop their redeployment in full stride, recover to a fully combat-ready stance, and prosecute a new and violent campaign against enemies in unfamiliar parts of Iraq. The epic Extension Campaign (Operation *Iron Sabre*) will long remain as one of the most novel military operations ever undertaken by an army division. It only capped, however, the extraordinary performance of Old Ironsides that itself remains a testimony to the professionalism and preparedness of the US Army in the beginning of the 21st century.

CHRONOLOGY

2001

November V Corps receives Joint Chiefs of Staff order to begin active planning for operations in southwest Asia, using a five-division base.

2002

July V Corps completes Operation Plan (OPLAN) *Decisive Victory*, its first plan involving 1st Armored Division and the first involving an attack all the way to Baghdad.

2003

February 7 1st Armored Division is dropped out of the initial deployment and assault plan for Operation *Iraqi Freedom*.

February 12 C Company, 2/6th Infantry deployed to serve as security for V Corps' headquarters.

February 20 1/41st Infantry deployed from Ft. Riley.

February 25 2/70th Armor deployed from Ft. Riley.

March 19 Operation *Iraqi Freedom* begins with V Corps attack across Kuwait–Iraq border.

April 7 1/13th Armor deployed from Ft. Riley.

April 9 1st Armored Division begins deployment from Germany to Kuwait.

April 14 1st Armored Division is assigned TF Baghdad mission by USCENTCOM.

April 28 The last 1st Armored Division cargo loads at Rotterdam and sails.

May 16–26 1st Armored Division assembles in Baghdad.

May 20 3d Brigade, 1st Armored Division completes deployment to Baghdad, forming with 3d Infantry Division.

May 29 1st Armored Division assumes mission as TF Baghdad.

June 2–11 Operation *Iron Dig* – excavation of the Al Sa'a Restaurant to determine if Saddam Hussein had been killed there.

June 15–29 Operation *Scorpion Sting* – combines raids, sweeps, cordons, and searches to gain intelligence, round up resistance, criminal and terrorist leaders and cells, simultaneously conducting engineering, humanitarian assistance, and stability operations.

July 14–18 Operation *Iron Mountain* – a significant force-protection stand-up throughout the former Ba'ath holiday period.

July 26–28 Operation *Iron Bounty* – documents captured during *Iron Mountain* lead to an operation to find and capture militia fighters.

August 8 1st Armored Division publishes its new campaign plan, estimating a one-year deployment requirement.

August 19 Bombing of the UN Headquarters.

August 26–September 9 Operation *Longstreet* – corps-level mission to disrupt sanctuaries that insurgents had established by operating in the boundary areas between divisional areas of operations in Iraq, where presence of US forces tended to be thin to non-existent.

September 6 Baghdad finishes 91 consecutive days of temperatures over 100°F (38°C).

October 10 Butler Range opens, thus providing gunnery training for all arms in the task force in a secure location away from the city.

October 19–21 Operation *Crossbow* – TF Baghdad support the Multinational Division Central-South (MND-CS) commander in response to civil disturbances by the "Mahdi Army" in Karbala.

November 12–27 Operation *Iron Hammer* – a major stabilization operation improvised from the task force's initial responses to increased attacks on its positions at the beginning of Ramadan.

November 14–30 "Early Retrograde" equipment, deemed non-essential to the current mission, departs Baghdad for Kuwait and home stations to prevent later congestion in the ports.

November 27 President of the United States George W. Bush visits Baghdad.

December 1–21 Operation *Iron Justice* targets a wide range of black marketeering and other criminal activities.

December 19–January 6, 2004 Operation *Iron Grip* – a cordon, search and raid effort designed to preemptively strike the enemy elements before their planned holiday attacks.

2004

January 8 36th Battalion Iraqi Civil Defense Corps (ICDC) activated.

January 8 C-5 transport hit by insurgent missile.

January 16–March 8 Operation *Iron Resolve* increases vigilance and security sweeps designed to cover the departure of 2d/82d Airborne and 3d Brigade, 1st Armored Division from Baghdad.

January 23 Transfer of Authority (TOA) of 2d/82d Airborne (by Division Artillery Combat Team – DCT, 1st Armored Division).

February 12 TOA with 3d/1st Armored Division (by 2d/1st Cavalry Division).

March 9–April 16 Operation *Iron Promise* – a lengthy period

of actions and follow-on developments to strengthen Baghdad security and bring a permanent posture of vigilance and effectiveness as the major units of TF Baghdad are relieved in place.

April 2–25 TOAs of remaining 1st Armored Division units:

1st Brigade	April 24	(by 39th Brigade)
2d Brigade	April 14	(by 3d/1st Cavalry Division)
4th Brigade	April 2	(by 4th/1st Cavalry Division)
Div Engineers	April 4	(by DE/1st Cavalry Division)
DCT	April 6	(by DCT/1st Cavalry Division)
2d ACR	April 10	(by 1st/1st Cavalry Division)
1st Arm Div	April 15	(by 1st Cavalry Division)

April 6 1st Armored Division halts redeployment movement.

April 6–8 TF Striker (2d Brigade) in combat, an Najaf.

April 9–12 TF Striker in combat, al-Kut.

April 16–July 7 Operation *Iron Sabre*.

April 29 Elements of 4/27th Field Artillery are attacked by a Vehicle Borne Improvised Explosive Device (VBIED) while escorting a TF Iron Claw team: eight killed in action (KIA), four wounded in action (WIA).

April 29 TF 1/37th Armor arrives at Karbala.

May 22 Karbala resistance ends, civil affairs operations continue.

June 18 The division's official redeployment recommences.

June 28 The Coalition Provisional Authority (CPA) and the governing council are dissolved and political authority passes to an interim government of Iraq.

July 5 1st Armored Division cases colors in Iraq.

July 8–29 1st Armored Division redeploys to German garrisons.

August 7 V Corps welcome home ceremony for 1st Armored Division.

2005

June 21 Old Ironsides reports "combat ready" to V Corps.

From the perch of an M2A2 Bradley Fighting Vehicle (BFV), this infantryman watches over a Traffic Control Point (TCP), with his M4 carbine and the ubiquitous civilian-type transceiver radio, barely discernible on the turret top to the right. He wears the Interceptor armored vest, showing the prominent throat protector "collar" and has an early "clip on" mount for the AN/PVS-14 monocular night-vision device on his Kevlar® helmet.

ENLISTMENT

The US Army abandoned military conscription in 1973, and spent some years developing a sophisticated system for the recruitment and administration of personnel. All the services had to organize new recruiting strategies and organizations. Until successive pay raises took place and made service more attractive to young men and women, the services struggled through the mid-1970s, recruiting substandard manpower in insufficient numbers. Only when standards of living and working, career opportunities, pay and benefits, and other less tangible factors had been improved, did the All-Volunteer Force begin to perform as expected, around 1977.

A key changeover for the All-Volunteer Force was the increased reliance upon women. The Gates Commission (convened to study the end of US conscription in peacetime) forecast a 10 percent female force, and during 1972–92, the US services saw a 2.1–11 percent growth in women recruits. Today, the new intake reportedly includes a 20 percent female component, thanks to the opening of all but close-combat military functions to women. The use of professional dedicated recruiters and modern advertising and sales techniques has proven equally important to success. The US Army, for example, employs today some 7,000 recruiters, or about 1 percent of its active duty force, operating out of 1,550 recruiting stations, to obtain its annual needs.

The basic system

Each service is responsible for its own recruitment and personnel management, although Congress and the Department of Defense (DoD) stipulate general requirements of standardization, rationalization, and equality. Each of the services operates recruiting commands charged with the conduct of the recruiting campaign, the processing of applicants (preliminary physical, mental, and moral/legal screening), and induction and transportation of the recruits. On arrival at training camps ("boot camp" is the US vernacular) the recruits undergo an intensive basic training of 8–16 weeks. After this basic training, the former recruits are handed over to the service personnel or manpower departments that classify the new servicemen and women for Military Occupational Specialty (MOS) and assign them either to a follow-on basic course in that specialty or to a unit (ship, station, organization) that will include specialty training in the initial assignment.

Targets on a small-arms range in the Butler Range Complex. The 56-sq. km (22-sq. mile) area has eight different types of ranges to support all organic weapons, to include tanks, artillery, and attack helicopters. The opening ceremony named the facility the Butler Range, after the first soldier of 1st Armored Division killed in action in the Iraq campaign, SGT Jacob Butler. It continues to operate to this day.

An M2A2 BFV fires its 25mm chaingun at the qualification range, Grafenwöhr, Germany. The mainstay of the mechanized infantry, the BFV served continuously in both urban and conventional combat roles, including considerable convoy and road-sweep escort missions. Many of them exchanged their European camouflage paint scheme for desert tan while in Iraq.

The only centralized function in the foregoing process is in the Defense-mandated Military Entrance Processing Stations (MEPS), which are jointly manned but administrated by the Army. At these centers physical and mental examinations (Armed Forces Vocational Aptitude Battery) are conducted to ensure that only suitable recruits are taken in by each of the services. These MEPS also function in wartime as mobilization and induction centers for conscripts.

Officer candidates receive the same induction, except for appointees to the service academies and those commissioned from the serving enlisted ranks. The service academies and the parent units handle these, using local military facilities as required for the entrance examinations. The basic training, career management, performance evaluations, assignments, continuing education and training, and other administrative measures such as pay, health, promotion, disciplinary, and retirement actions are all encompassed in the personnel management or manpower systems operated by the specific military services.

Recruiting, induction, and basic training of officers and enlisted personnel for the Army Reserve and National Guard are performed by the active duty recruit commands, and the personnel are turned over to the reserve component command after completion of the prescribed training and/or active duty period of service. A Total Force System (TFS) has been in place for 20 years, wherein the reserve conducts its own local operations and unit training regimen, but all matters of personnel management and schools assignment are controlled by the active component of the military service. For personnel leaving active duty, their recruitment into the reserve forces is managed in a two-tier approach: (1) the releasing service offers the relevant reserve appointment opportunity; and (2) the recruit command station at the home of record/return of the discharged man or woman makes contact for possible reserve service opportunities. An honorably discharged enlisted person has the right to apply for reinstatement to active duty without loss of grade or seniority for 90 days after discharge, subject to the needs of the releasing service.

The enlisted force

To enlist in the US forces, a man or woman must:

- be between the ages of 17 and 35 (under 18 requires parental consent or proof of emancipation); by 2006, because of wartime exigencies, the maximum age for enlistment was 42, with a signing bonus of $40,000 for new active duty recruits and $20,000 for reservists.

- be a US citizen or resident alien.
- pass medical and minimal intelligence and physical fitness standards.
- have no police record outside of minor infractions.

Enlistment contracts run from two to six years in duration, depending upon the service and the type of program or specialty offered to the recruit. Each service may impose additional requirements for special programs. There are few openings for non-graduates of high school. Well-qualified recruits are given incentive packages promising a particular specialty, training, and/or geographic assignment. Women remain excluded from ground combat (infantry, artillery, armor) and submarine branches.

Assignment policies vary by service and specialty, but regulations of the DoD put limitations on the number of days per year a soldier, sailor, or airman may be assigned away from home station and the frequency of assignments to overseas bases (e.g. a limit of 400 days' individual service away from home station per two years, and minimum rest periods for units between overseas deployments). The normal assignment is for three years, reduced to one or two for so-called "hardship" posts, such as the Aleutian Islands, Antarctica, or other isolated locations. For married personnel ordered to overseas duty without family, a one-year tour is prescribed.

The normal career pattern for the enlisted man or woman will combine periods of assignment in and out of specialty. There is advanced training in further specialties or general subjects – e.g. leadership and non-commissioned officer (NCO) courses – and encouragement to obtain civilian education through off-duty programs and the limited amount of service programs that detail enlisted personnel to college

The demands of a modern army require almost all personnel to understand information technology, operating not only the usual laptop computers, seen here in the division operations center, but also myriad specialized derivatives used in administrative, logistics, and ordnance applications.

courses. Officer programs remain open to enlisted persons who qualify by age, education, aptitude, and command recommendation. Several key specialties and hazardous duty assignments bring special monthly pay augmentation as well as lump-sum bonus payments for signing and completing minimum periods of service.

A complete career through retirement consists of consecutive enlistment contracts (there is a provision for "broken time" or exit/reentry from active service) culminating in at least 20 years' service. After this period the service member may request retirement at 50 percent basic pay (i.e. not including special allowances), plus 2.5 percent pay for each year over 20 served to a maximum of 75 percent base pay. However, consecutive reenlistment contracts require advancement to minimum pay grades by specified time frames, such that Grade 6 will be reached by retirement. Retirement in lesser grades may occur due to medical or disability retirement or a sequence of "broken time" enlistments where the individual accumulated the required 20 years but had insufficient time in grade for advancement to Grade 6.

Promotions are based upon a combination of minimum time in grade, qualification in specialty for that grade, special schooling, qualification for or completion of required courses, command recommendation, and annual ratings or fitness reports (for upper grades). Promotions to junior enlisted grades are made by the service personnel management system, using criteria of time in grade plus performance marks, as well as the vacancies for grade by specialty in the service. Promotions to the top three or four grades of enlisted persons are effected by nine-person promotion boards consisting of officers and senior enlisted persons.

TRAINING

Every soldier receives additional specialty training after completion of recruit training. In many cases, this training takes place at the branch schools of the Army: infantry at Ft. Benning, armor at Ft. Knox, artillery at Ft. Sill, engineers at Ft. Leonard Wood, signals at Ft. Gordon, and so forth. Most courses extend from 12 to 16 weeks for qualifying basic soldiers in their MOS, and equivalent courses train senior enlisted personnel in expert and management subject areas. The newly qualified soldiers proceed to their assigned organizations, where they undertake unit-level training to integrate properly into the required level of teamwork and expertise for military operations.

During 2002 more signs began to appear that signaled impending US military action against Iraq. The American government had already demonstrated its desire to settle direct and latent threats to security in the aftermath of the September 11, 2001 attacks on US soil. Thus, even before the

The tank commander (left) and loader man with their respective .50-cal. and 7.62mm machine guns on an M1A1 tank. None of the tanks of the 1st Armored Division changed out of their European camouflage paint scheme for this campaign. The men wear Interceptor vests and commercial ballistic eyewear. Their M4 carbines remain ready to use, the commander studies his map; the spent cartridge cases indicate he has used his machine gun recently.

campaign against Afghanistan culminated in the establishment of a friendly interim government there, planning continued for removing the dictatorship government of Iraq, with the hope of stabilizing the region.

For the officers and enlisted soldiers of the 1st Armored Division, training and other preparations became more intensive and focused through 2002. Whether a unilateral US action or a large-scale international campaign on the scale of the 1990–91 Gulf conflict was approaching, there seemed little doubt that the division would be involved. The intransigence of Saddam Hussein and the determination of the US government to resolve the situation meant that major combat operations would be required to defeat Iraqi forces and occupy the country. Old Ironsides was the last of the conventional US armored divisions left in service after the defense draw-down of the 1990s (although 1st Cavalry and 4th Infantry divisions had similar configurations), and it was inevitable that it would be at the center of the campaign. The division and other organizations earmarked in the planning dedicated more attention to troop training in personal and crew-served weapons, individual tactical training, and preparing for the demands of fighting under chemical and biological warfare conditions.

Various options for the invasion and occupation of Iraq were studied by the theater and national commanders, but the "Iron Soldiers" at their posts in Germany and Ft. Riley, Kansas (the home base of the 3d Brigade Combat Team – BCT), concerned themselves with required training and readiness tasks that would be needed for any outcome. Late in 2002, some of the plans considered using both the 3d Infantry Division and 1st Armored Division as the leading elements of the V Corps' attack, supported by the 101st Airborne Division. Other major units, like the 4th Infantry Division, 1st Cavalry Division, and 82d Airborne Division would reinforce or perform supporting missions for V Corps. However, by February 7, 2003, V Corps' force lists had been stripped of many units and revised plans called for a starkly reduced attack force, with reinforcements to be "rolled" into the theater after combat began. The simultaneous initiation of combat operations and RSOI (Reception, Staging, Onward movement and Integration of forces using "force packages" or "modules" [portions of units designated for movement together in assigned airlift and sealift groups]) had no real precedent and left units not yet deployed to the theater in deep uncertainty.

Amid this turmoil, the commander of 1st Armored Division, Major General (MG) Ricardo S. Sanchez, decided that his own staff would shield the rest of the division from the ambiguities of the planning, thereby leaving the Iron Soldiers to their scheduled training, logistics, and personnel readiness tasks:

> This division and the corps have done exercises over the course of last year at a rate that I never did as a brigade commander. I never experienced that while I was over here before, either – then, you

had one major exercise a year and that's what we all shot for. Now, we've had major command post exercises at the division or corps level about every quarter. That's what it's averaged out to. Being able to exercise the division in the context of a corps and within the battle rhythms of a corps is crucial, because it drives the tempo of operations all the way down to the battalion. Laying out the communications architecture for the division was a challenge during [Exercise] Victory Focus and then on the [Exercise] Warfighter. Therefore, we put out as a challenge for ourselves to be able to lay out a comms architecture for the division over a couple hundred kilometers to see whether we could make it work. So during one of my division-level training events, that's exactly what we did. We laid out all of our command and communications nodes all the way from Giessen down to Baumholder, right across the division garrison area, in our home stations, and tried to make that work. That's 120 miles, and it was challenging. We had never done that before. Then we displaced the comms and reestablished them. We took tremendous lessons from that. We changed our entire training approach for Hohenfels and Grafenwöhr, based on the challenges we foresaw. Our movements from home station tested our deployment capability and our ability to control those movements. We loaded out the entire brigade team, packing everything that we owned, stood up the base support battalion and area support group deployment support activities, processed the units for deployments, moved the brigade combat teams in force packages to their forward deployed locations – APOD or SPOD [Aerial or Sea Port of Departure], whichever we were simulating – and went through combat power building at that location. Then we did integration training at Grafenwöhr. Then we road marched to the tactical assembly area at Hohenfels and lived in the field for sixty days – something we hadn't done before.

M109A6 Paladin 155mm self-propelled howitzers of 2d Battalion, 3d Field Artillery are silhouetted during a maintenance day in their Forward Operating Base (FOB). Most of the artillery remained idle during the urban campaign and the soldiers served as infantrymen, only to resume conventional operations a year later against the al-Sadr rising in the summer of 2004.

The capstone event in the predeployment training process was the division's "2-minute drill" (the special play sequence devised by US professional football teams in the final moments of a game). Essentially, this was a division-wide gunnery exercise involving all major weapons systems, including crew-served and individual small arms. The training was completed in three weeks and required the most intensive use of weapons ranges in the recent history of the division. The Division Support Command (DISCOM) not only supported the supply and maintenance of all weapons systems, but also qualified over 1,800 of its own soldiers on their individual weapons.

The true heroes of the 2-minute drill were the personnel of the division ammunition office. They were given the monumental task of ensuring that all range ammunition requirements were completed satisfactorily. For nearly 30 days, the office handled requests, issued ammunition, and processed the turn-in of live and residual ammunition.

M1A1 Abrams main battle tanks of 1st Armored Division on the firing line at Grafenwöhr Range Complex, Germany. Despite dire predictions and critiques, the tank remained essential for urban combat. Its precision fire control minimized "collateral" damage during firefights, and the 120mm cannon projectiles would hit and explode on their intended targets, not ricochet or penetrate into adjoining buildings, as did the machine-gun and light cannon projectiles of other weapons systems. Note the louvered thermal identification panel carried on the turret side. In combat it is mounted on either side of the turret face.

An urban "combat stack" of infantrymen prepares to enter a building during a search and clearing operation. Each soldier has assigned sectors of observation and movement once entry begins. Visible non-standard equipment items include knee and ankle pads, ballistic glasses, knee clipboards, and thigh-strap pistol holsters.

Through their responsive and flexible efforts, every ammunition requirement was met.

Immediately following the 2-minute drill, the division moved into a dedicated maintenance period at the organizational and Direct Support (DS) levels to repair vehicles and weapon systems. This period was intended to last just over two weeks, but it was compressed to meet the deployment schedule. The DISCOM concentrated its resources on maintaining the equipment of division units and deferring maintenance on its organic equipment. As a direct result of this effort, the division successfully loaded 8,500 pieces of rolling stock on ships with fewer than 60 pieces deadlined (requiring repair or parts to return to service). The division materiel readiness section tracked the readiness status of equipment being out-loaded daily, identified required maintenance, and determined the repair parts that would be needed on arrival in Kuwait.

Despite the intensive preparations conducted by his command, Gen Sanchez still had concerns at the end of February. The problems endemic to urban operations remained vexing and he had little confidence that the logistics sustainability of the force had been

prepared adequately. In his eyes the logistical defects experienced in the previous Gulf War (1990–91) had not been remedied. One could still run out of fuel after covering 300km (186 miles), despite the promises of "just-in-time" logistics doctrine. Of one thing, Sanchez could be certain – little time remained. His liaison officers at V Corps reported to him on Sunday, February 9 that the ground combat phase could begin as early as the period March 5–15. Thus there was a minimalist option: sending only the 3d Infantry Division and the corps attack aviation into action, with the 101st Airborne and 3d ACR following later, when completely integrated. There was no way to get 1st Armored Division into the initial attack force. Whether it participated in conventional high-intensity combat or Stability Operations and Support Operations (SOSO) in the aftermath of the fighting remained to be determined. The next day, Old Ironsides was ordered to provide a mechanized infantry company to V Corps to serve as its command post security element. It seemed like the fight was drawing farther away from the division, despite its extensive preparations for deployment. C Company, 2/6th Infantry thus became the first 1st Armored Division unit tasked to deploy to Kuwait and the edge of battle.

Sanchez's other concern was the prospect of urban combat. Training at platoon and company level alone would not suffice for the scale and duration of the missions at hand. Clearing rooms and buildings remained distinct problems from the need to synchronize the urban battlefield at the battalion through division levels. In an urban context the technical and tactical advantages of a first-rate combat force cannot easily be brought to bear against a third-rate one, and the presence of civilians compounds this problem. During February 5–8, 1st Armored Division conducted staff seminar planning under V Corps auspices for Urban Operations (UO) training. Directed by BG Fred D. Robinson, the assistant division commander (maneuver), the 2d Brigade provided the

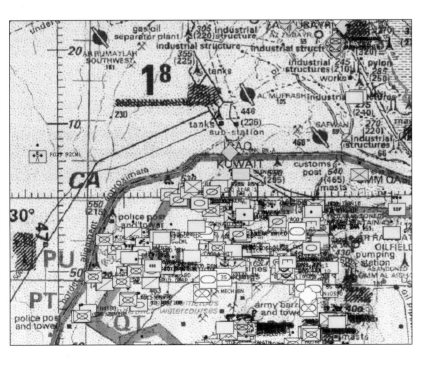

The Blue Force Tracker display of coalition forces on the eve of the invasion of Iraq. Taken at 2008hrs on March 19, 2003, it shows the density of units amassed along the border before crossing into Iraq. These and other real-time electronic systems facilitated efficient communication, command, and control, and thereby avoided friendly-fire situations undesirable in modern operations.

staff to plan and execute the simulated operations. Working groups analyzed the FOB concept at brigade and division levels and studied how urban raids could be conducted in a variety of scenarios from such bases. As a result, the seminar developed an extensive series of tactics, techniques, and procedures. These incorporated battlefield operating systems for each phase of the FOB and raid concepts.

As the division leadership assessed the challenges of urban operations, the long-awaited deployment orders arrived. The Joint Staff ordered the deployment of the movement "module" containing the 1st Armored Division on February 28, echoed on March 1 and March 3 by US Army and USCENTCOM orders to deploy the division and receive it in Kuwait. After over a year of dedicated training and preparations, Old Ironsides was going to war, not far from where it had triumphed a mere 12 years before, in the 1991 Gulf War to liberate Kuwait.

DAILY LIFE

In order to establish security in Baghdad, the units in a given district operated out of their FOBs, each of which had to be fortified, patrolled, and secured. This rotating duty consisted of guarding the perimeter walls or fences using static guard posts, manned in random fashion except in the case of alerts. Roving patrols outside the perimeter covered approach routes and potential assembly areas for attackers. A quick-response force remained at the ready inside the FOB to deal with immediate threats.

From their FOB deployment posture, various elements of the battalions and companies could depart and return to perform the daily tasks required in their assigned neighborhoods. Static guard positions covered the fixed facilities that required security, mounted and foot patrols covered foot and traffic routes, and TCPs were established as part of the effort to regulate and monitor movement of enemy forces and weapons. At the beginning of the occupation of Baghdad, the extensive looting raised the number of positions that US forces needed to protect, a demand that easily exceeded the troops available, leaving few for use on other tasks. These facilities included public buildings, key commercial sites – such as gasoline stations and cultural centers – down to the level of municipal museums, some of which no longer contained any artifacts in wake of the earlier looting.

Gen John M. Keane, the Army Vice Chief of Staff, tests the line service in an early FOB mess tent. With the change of deployments of US Army units to annual rotations, the need for quality of life improvements in the camps led to massive construction and modernization efforts, including the provision of full-service cafeteria ("dining facility") and fast-food services.

Living conditions

The evident fact that the US forces would have to remain in Iraq for an indefinite period forced a concerted effort to improve the living standards and morale of those forces. The troops already suffered under appalling conditions of heat and dust in the summer of 2003, and the emerging news that they would not be returning home very soon tended to lay their spirits low. Soldiers would be granted, as much as possible, mid tour-of-duty leave out of the country, while maintaining minimum 90 percent unit strength for mission readiness. A concerted furlough program would take as many soldiers as possible to rest centers

in Kuwait and Qatar (5,400 troops was the goal) and shorter breaks in Green Zone recreational facilities in the city. The FOBs would be reduced in number and refurbished from temporary to "enduring" standards with habitability, recreation, communications, entertainment, and food services greatly enhanced. By the end of the deployment, six new major encampments replaced the FOBs, located away from the city center. The soldiers and engineers of TF 1st Armored Division began the construction of 26 semi-permanent FOBs, replacing the 46 temporary sites occupied in April–May, which consisted simply of the bases, government compounds, and palaces of the deposed regime. Usually built on the site of a temporary FOB, these were built to standards that far exceeded the relative squalor of the temporary camps.

The construction procedure followed similar patterns throughout Baghdad. Engineers delivered thousands of tons of gravel for the roads and then provided, sometimes with local Iraqi contractors, the outer defensive walls, guard towers, barracks, armories, guardrooms, headquarters, and maintenance buildings for the FOB. Water and electrical supplies and sanitary facilities came on line at the same time. By September 2003, formal dining facilities had opened.

Engineers turned to paving new roads leading into the FOBs and some also within them. Air conditioning units were installed as soon as they could be obtained and telephone exchanges, internet cafés, and post exchanges emerged in October. Eventually the cots in the barracks gave way to real beds and mattresses. By the end of October, the 26 rebuilt FOBs had almost all received the desired standard, as expressed by the division commander of TF 1st Armored Division, encompassing: force protection; newspapers; recreation equipment; fitness centers; recreation and rest center access; post exchange access; cots (later beds); ice; water; laundry; food services; telephones; cyber cafés; tents; floors; power; air conditioning; chemical latrines; waste management; showers; vector control (mosquitoes, etc.)

Each of these categories had detailed criteria. For instance, the telephone standard in 1st Armored Division was one 15-minute call per week per soldier. To attain this, the division provided a combination of official telephone lines, commercial satellite links (AT&T and Thulaya), cell phones (MCI), and commercial landline phone banks (AT&T). By January, the FOB construction program was focused on building eight "Enduring" or "Expeditionary" (i.e. permanent or five to ten years'

ABOVE LEFT **One of the largest FOBs supported 2d ACR in east Baghdad. The Muleskinner FOB included Redcatcher Field, named for the call-sign of the regiment's air cavalry squadron, co-located with the service squadron at Muleskinner. This sprawling compound was the Iraqi base al-Rastimiya, site of the Iraqi war college.**

ABOVE RIGHT **In his first visit to Iraq, US President George W. Bush landed secretly at BIAP on November 27, 2003, and attended the Thanksgiving dinner arranged for selected groups of soldiers from the units of the task force. President Bush wears the standard army recreational jacket, emblazoned with the 1st Armored Division patch. Ambassador Bremmer and the corps commander, LTG Sanchez, the latter with holster empty, flank him.**

lifespan) camps designed for continuous operation for the foreseeable future in Baghdad. Engineers of TF 1st Armored Division managed an $800 million project to build these camps for the occupation by the incoming 1st Cavalry Division, slated to arrive after mid-March, 2004. The camps introduced a quantum improvement to the FOB system by improving soldier quality of life with additional security by locating to the outskirts of the city. The old FOBs reverted to the Iraqi government for use as ICDC, army, or police bases or other uses. On November 27, 2003, 1st Armored Division hosted and facilitated the surprise visit of George W. Bush, Dr. Condoleezza Rice, Mr. L. Paul Bremmer, and LTG Sanchez, with members of the White House Press Corps for Thanksgiving Day activities at the Baghdad International Airport (BIAP) dining facility. The division Public Affairs Section coordinated coverage for network television of soldiers' reactions to President Bush's visit. Wearing an army workout jacket emblazoned with Old Ironsides' patch, Mr. Bush spoke warmly of the division, as well as 2d ACR and 82d Airborne divisions.

APPEARANCE AND EQUIPMENT

Soldiers assigned to TF Baghdad used an almost baffling array of uniform and equipment items, with standardization required only for combat functions undertaken outside the FOBs. Additionally, the troops to this day have continued to blend in commercial field equipment (from companies such as Blackhawk or Brigade Quartermaster) or variations of military-issue items, in some instances purchased by their own organizations for use on deployment.

Soldiers deployed to Baghdad wore the Battle Dress Uniform (BDU) in desert camouflage, but most equipment items remained in the standard olive green or woodland camouflage of previous eras. Issued since 1981, the uniform consists of matching hat, shirt, and trousers and the three-tone desert camouflage replaced the six-color "chocolate chip" uniform worn in the previous Gulf War. A soft field hat (the "boonie") also was available in all the patterns, serving particularly well for personnel exposed to the harsh daylight conditions. It features a standard-width quilted stitched brim, chinstrap, and camouflage band. In the winter months, troops wore a matched camouflage version of the venerable M65 field jacket. A rough leather desert combat boot, cut to the familiar style of the black leather boot, finished off the uniform, and here many commercial brands could be seen in use, as the government engaged several vendors to fill its clothing outlets.

Most of the standard web gear was shelved during occupation duty, because the soldiers operated out of nearby FOBs and rarely stayed away for 24 hours. Thus, the rucksacks, suspenders, belts, and canteens gave way in most cases to the use of body armor as a load carrier, festooned with gear held on by straps, clips, and carabineers of all

Soldiers of the 2/6th Infantry prepare for action during a raid near the Green Zone. While all wear Interceptor vests with SAPI plates, other equipment varies. The helmet scope mounts are the strap-on type, all have flashlight pointers for their M4 carbines, and the man on the right also has an M203 grenade launcher and laser pointer attached to his weapon. The ALICE-type magazine and grenade pouches are attached directly to the Interceptor vests, instead of using web gear, thus minimizing bulk and possible snags.

kinds, Velcro fasteners, and in some cases combinations of harnesses and M67 pistol belts. Gas masks and other specialized gear usually appeared only when use of tear gas or riot control agents could be anticipated. In the appalling heat conditions of Iraq, the soldier's load felt double its weight. Few units standardized the way equipment was worn, but personnel leaving the FOB for any reason usually had the required uniform, helmet, body armor, weapon, first aid kit, ammo magazines/pouches, water supply, ballistic eyewear, polypropylene neck protector, and gloves.

The rifle configurations rivaled personal equipment in variety. The M4 and M4A carbine version of the M16A2 service rifle were carried with a variety of attachments: scopes, laser, or flashlight pointers; M203 grenade launcher; Advanced Combat Optical Gunsight (ACOG) reflexive sight or 4× scope; and, for special operations, hand grips and sound suppressors. Units of the National Guard and Army Reserve frequently brought the older M16A2 to the campaign. Soldiers used various commercial and military slings to hang them in a two- or three-point configuration for quick use on patrol and at checkpoints. The Personnel Armor System Ground Troops (PASGT) helmet (also known as the "Kevlar") was the standard infantry helmet. Available since the 1980s, it provides ballistic protection from fragments of exploding munitions. It consists, like most infantry helmets, of a protective shell and a suspension system that fits comfortably on the user. The shell features multiple levels of Kevlar® aramid fiber. The suspension harness uses a two-point chinstrap with an open chin cup and two adjustable buckles and a single snap fastener on the left. When properly sized and adjusted, the suspension provides a minimum half-inch between the head and inner helmet surface for ventilation and to create a distance from impacts deforming the shell. A cloth cover provides several camouflage patterns and a band is furnished, to which camouflage materials may be attached. The current PASGT helmet made of Kevlar® 29 weighs 3.1–4.2lb (1.4–1.9kg) but a lighter (3.7lb/1.7kg max.) Army Combat Helmet with improved suspension was introduced after the start of the campaign. The AN/PVS-14 monocular night-vision device attaches via a helmet mount to the PASGT helmet. When attached to the mount, the goggle lowers directly in front of the user's eyes or flips up out of the way. The goggle features a 50-hour operating period on two AA size batteries, weighing merely 13.5oz (382g).

Body armor consisted of two types during the initial stages of the 2003–04 campaign. Because of the critical nature of the Baghdad

ABOVE LEFT **Soldiers practice firing the M249 SAW at the Butler Range Complex under the direction of a senior NCO wearing the combat patch of the 82d Airborne Division. One soldier, perhaps a new arrival, wears the standard forest camouflage battle dress, the others the standard desert pattern. All wear desert boots. The only non-standard gear in evidence is the knee and elbow padding worn by the instructor.**

ABOVE RIGHT **Soldiers of the 2d ACR on night patrol, the man on the left displaying the AN/PVS-14 monocular night-vision device in raised position, out of use. On the right, one sees how the Interceptor Outer Tactical Vest (OTV) carries the magazine and grenade pouches of the standard ALICE web gear system.**

This captain, posing in a favored photo venue, the Iraqi Crossed Swords Monument, wears the PASGT armored vest, which has a removable three-quarter collar, pivoting shoulder pads, two front pockets, two grenade hangers and rifle butt patches at the front shoulder area. He also wears ALICE-type suspenders, and an M67 pistol belt.

mission, the early PASGT vests used by non-infantry soldiers were replaced by the superior Interceptor system by the midpoint of TF 1st Armored Division's deployment.

The PASGT vest replaced the older vinyl and ballistic plate combination that dated from the M1969 Fragmentation Protective Body Armor. The ballistic filler consists of 13 plies of treated (water-repellent) aramid Kevlar® 29 fabric. The inner and outer cover, shoulder pads, and front closure flap of the vest are water-repellent ballistic nylon cloth. The outer cover is in woodland camouflage and the inner cover is olive green. The vest has a removable three-quarter collar, pivoting shoulder pads, two front pockets, two grenade hangers and rifle butt patches at the front shoulder area. The front flap and pocket flaps have hook and loop fastener tape closures. The PASGT vest improved on previous protection against fragments.

The Interceptor Multi-Threat Body Armor System consists of two components: the OTV and Small Arms Protective Inserts, or "SAPI plates." This system features removable throat and groin protectors, as well as front and back removable SAPI plates, which can stop 7.62mm rounds. It weighs 16.4lb (7.5kg); each of the two inserts weighs 4lb (1.8kg), and the OTV weighs 8.4lb (3.8kg). OTV's Kevlar® weave can stop a 9mm bullet. In addition, the strapping and Velcro fasteners of the Interceptor can be attached to personal equipment. The SAPI plates are ceramic. The Armor Protection Enhancement System (APES) adds sections to protect the neck, arms, and groin. The Deltoid Extension protects the sides of the ribcage and shoulders, at a cost of an additional 5lb (2.3kg) in weight, less ventilation, and limits to body movement. The US Army selected the IC-F3S portable transceiver for the new "Soldier Intercom" in 1998. AN/PRC-119F SINGARS VHF radios also served at the squad level, but once again, a variety of commercial transceivers and cellular phones came into use in Baghdad. The ubiquitous commercial item of personal gear was the Camelbak® hydration pack, carried slung in the small of the back with an over-shoulder supply tube providing easy access to water in much greater quantity than the issue canteens, which virtually disappeared from use. Soldiers also carried an array of ballistic glasses, knee/elbow/ankle pads, or shields and gloves made of Kevlar®

or other tough materials for the daily work of urban patrolling amid rubble, steel, broken glass, and contaminants. In addition, commercial equivalents of military-issue magazines and pouches and the usual array of survival and mountaineering equipment all came into use according to individual needs, and were made accessible due to access to internet and postal communications while on campaign.

BELIEF AND BELONGING

For the entire period of its service in Iraq during 2003–04, Old Ironsides served the CPA and US forces, first in the stabilization and security operations in the capital city, followed by its Extension Campaign, fought to reestablish order when the al-Sadr rising threatened the restoration of sovereignty to an Iraqi provisional government. The designation of the 1st Armored Division as TF Baghdad underlined the critical nature of the assignment, for Baghdad loomed as the vital node where the coalition forces would make or break their effort to restore order in Iraq and complete the move toward democratic rule.

In doing so, the division and its Iron Soldiers, with the reinforcing organizations that joined it in TF Baghdad, operated with initial handicaps that would be overcome only by gaining experience. The myriad tasks facing an armored division in Baghdad, so recently sent to the theater after detailed preparations for high-intensity combat, almost defy description. A broken city lay at its feet, occupied by inhabitants thoroughly demoralized by the shock of war and occupation, lacking any level of experience in self-government and self-sufficiency to make a concerted effort at rebuilding.

In many respects, the startling change in missions could only have been faced by an organization so thoroughly trained and cohesive. The 1st Armored Division was confident in and responsive to its leadership at all levels,

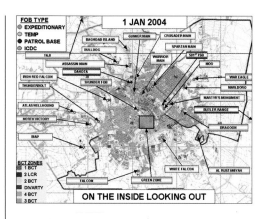

This briefing chart of TF 1st Armored Division includes most of the FOBs established in Baghdad during the first half-year of the occupation. The 3d Infantry Division had occupied 46 initial FOBs in April–May 2003. For the most part, they were Iraqi palaces, and defense and internal security unit garrisons but included, for example, one amusement park by the river. The US command reclassified them as "temporary" FOBs when it became clear that the mission was enduring. By the end of October 2003, 26 FOBs had been refurbished as new FOBs, also considered "temporary" in plans, with a further eight earmarked for reconstruction as "expeditionary" or "enduring" bases, designed for a five to ten year lifespan.

and capable of mobilizing and focusing the widest capabilities of military and civilian organizations that became available. The intensive training effort oriented to high-intensity combat that the 1st Armored Division followed until its deployment from Germany and the United States ironically proved essential for the vastly different challenges it faced, however unforeseen they may have been.

The 1st Armored soldiers saw the longest deployment of any division in Iraq. TF 1st Armored Division also comprised the largest divisional task force in US Army history. At its peak strength, there were more than 39,000 soldiers formed in the organization, which counted up to 14 brigades and numerous small units. The task force secured Baghdad's roughest neighborhoods and initially brought stability to the city and its surrounding countryside. It set up a local security apparatus and engaged the native leadership in order to found the grass roots civic organizations and leadership that alone would bring successful conversion of the city to self-rule. Not only did the task force provide security for over 5 million inhabitants, but it also facilitated a large number of reconstruction projects. In doing so, TF 1st Armored Division exceeded any previous US military effort at nation building.

All these accomplishments came in rapid succession to an organization boasting no experience or preparation in these types of operation. Rather, the soldiers and their attachment comrades reached into themselves and drew upon their training, discipline, pride, dedication to duty, physical readiness, and fighting spirit to adapt to the novel conditions and dangers of Baghdad missions, and executed them with unparalleled success. For the soldiers and their leaders, failure remained unthinkable.

These same collective and individual qualities of the soldiers of TF 1st Armored Division came into play with the epic Extension Campaign of April–July 2004. There exists no parallel event in US military history for the change in mission and turnaround of the division from its April 2004 redeployment to sustained combat in a matter of days. At the time that the task force first turned to deal with the al-Sadr rising, its troops and equipment extended from Baghdad through Kuwait to Germany and the United States. Having virtually relinquished the Baghdad mission, TF 1st Armored Division had packed and convoyed for its home stations.

However, in short order, the division swung back into action. Units still in Baghdad fought the rising alongside the relief unit, the 1st Cavalry Division. The first combat forces sortied to take back control of an Najaf and al-Kut in mere days. In a matter of weeks, the division – including entire units returned from home stations in Germany – scoured the 17,000 sq. km (6,562 sq. miles) of the new area of operations to quash the rising, restore coalition land routes, and bring order throughout. Even before the last insurgents were routed, the task force brought relief to embattled communities and began the reconstruction of battered cities and roadways, at the same time constructing a new set of FOBs that reestablished the coalition military balance.

Those mission successes and achievements did not come without cost. During the campaign of Operation *Iraqi Freedom* One, 130 soldiers of TF

1st Armored Division lost their lives while serving in Iraq and 1,111 were wounded in combat. Since March 20, 2003, elements of the 1st Armored Division have provided an almost continuous presence in Iraq. In terms of major unit deployments, the 3d Brigade deployed to Iraq from Ft. Riley, Kansas, once again in February 2005 for Operation *Iraqi Freedom* Three, after only nine months back in the United States. There they attached to the 3d Infantry Division, once again serving with TF Baghdad. The 1st and 2d brigades, with attachments, deployed to Kuwait in December 2005, and Iraq in January 2006. Other task forces and detachments have served in the interim, as well as numerous individual replacements and augmenters sent to Iraq. The recognition achieved by organizations and individuals demonstrated the key contributions made by the task force in a critical period of US military actions. Soldiers received some 3,400 individual awards of at least the Bronze Star/Air Medal level, including 118 Bronze Stars with combat "V" and higher. The 1st and 2d brigades and the 2d ACR earned Presidential Unit Citations for the campaign, and Valorous Unit Awards went to 3d and 4th brigades, 2d/82d Airborne Division, DISCOM and the Headquarters and Headquarters Company, and the units "task organized" under the brigades and 2d ACR. Meritorious Unit Awards were earned by the Division Artillery (DIVARTY), Division Engineers, 141st Signal Battalion, 501st Military Police Battalion, and the 501st Military Intelligence Battalion, except for those subordinate units attached to the previously cited organizations.

When Old Ironsides cased its colors in Iraq on July 5, 2004, its commander summed up the record to his soldiers:

> Fifteen months ago, Iron Soldiers of 1st Armored Division and Dragoons of 2nd Armored Cavalry Regiment formed a task force and set out to make the world safer for their fellow Americans and provide an opportunity for the Iraqi people to be free. They did that. The colors we have just cased are part of what defines us. Sometime soon we will add a battle streamer to those colors. That simple strip of silk will represent many things. It will represent more than a year of your life. It will represent your 130 fellow soldiers who gave their lives for this mission and who made the journey home ahead of us. It will represent your great courage in battle. It will represent your remarkable stamina over these past 15 months. It will represent your unshakable honor tested in the most complex environment imaginable. It will represent your immeasurable sacrifice and that of your families. Forever more it will represent you. These are truly your colors now. You have earned the right to stand tall behind them.

ON CAMPAIGN

Under the operational control of the 3d Infantry Division, the major units of the 1st Armored Division arrived and took over their sectors from May 16, 2003. Also in place were the newly arrived 2d Armored (Light) Cavalry Regiment and the 2d/82d Airborne Division. The respective 3d brigades exchanged duties in al-Mansour district northeast of BIAP.

The deployment task organization of 1st Armored Division before arrival in Baghdad shows its composition as a heavy division: three brigades with five armor and four infantry battalions, the fourth brigade of aviation, as well as DIVARTY, cavalry, air defense artillery, engineers, and support command, and separate battalions of military intelligence, signal, MP, chemical, and civil affairs, 315th Psyops Company, 305th Reserve Operations Center, and the division headquarters.

DEPLOYMENT TASK ORGANIZATION

1 (XX)

1 (X)	**2 (X)**	**3 (X)**	**4 (X)**	**DIV (X)**	**1-1 (II)**	**1-4 (II)**	**DIV (X)**
1-37 AR	1-6 IN	1-13 AR(Attach	1-501 AVN		3x GRD TRP	3/D/1-4 (GS)	EN BDE
2-37 AR	2-6 IN (-)	3ID)	2-501 AVN	DIVARTY	2x AIR TRP	4/D/1-4 (GS)	878 EN BN (CBT HVY)
1-36 IN	1-35 AR	2-70 AR(Attach 3	127 ASB(-)	1-94 FA (MLRS)(-)	B/127(-) (DS) (CST)	2/3rd Sec	479 EN BN (C)(M)
BRT	BRT	ID)	A/3-58 ATS (DS)		2/B/1-4 ADA (DS)	Sentinel (GS)	842 EN CO (CSE)
2-3 FA + Q36	4-27 FA + Q36	1-41 IN (VC TCF)	4/69 CHEM (DS)		1/3rd Sec Sentinel (GS)		526 EN DET (TRN)
A/1-4 ADA (DS)	D/1-94(TAB)	BRT	2 DET/7 W SQ		GSR/C/501 MI (DS)		518 EN DET (TRN)
1st Sec Sentinel(GS)	B/1-4 ADA (-)(DS)	4-1 FA	TACP/1 ASOS		A/16 EN BN		
16 EN BN (-)	1/D/1-4 ADA (DS)	C/1-4 ADA (DS)	2/D/1-4 (DS)		6/69 CHEM		
501 FSB (-)DS	2nd SEC Sentinel	70 ENG(-)	SEC/1/A/141		SEC/1/A/141 SIG		
A/501 MI (DS)	(GS)	125 FSB (DS)	SIG (SEN) (DS)		(SEN) (DS)		
1/69 CHEM	40 EN BN	o/o C/501 MI					
1DET/1ASOS	47 FSB (-)(DS)	596 SIG CO					
55 FAST 1	B (+) /501 MI (DS)	10 ASOS(-)					
SEC/1/A/141 SIG	2/69 CHEM	DECON PLT					
(SEN) (DS)	2DET/1ASOS	(TDA))					
	55 FAST 2						
	SEC/1/B/141 SIG						
	(SEN) (DS)						

DISCOM (II)	**MI**	**MI (II)**	**MP (I (-))**	**(I)**	**CA (II)**	**ROC (II)**	**DIV**
123MSB	HHC	HHC	HQ/501	3/69 CHEM (DS	HQ (DTAC)		DTAC
TF AMMO:	C/501	A/141 (-)	1/501	To ENG BDE)	1 TPD (DS		DMAIN
LAO (OPCON	D (-) /501	B/141 (-)	2/501 (GS)	HQ/69	1-1 Cav)		DREAR FWD
FOR MVMT)		C/141	4/501 (GS)	5/69	2 TPD (DS		HHC
95 Maint Co			5/501		28CT)		8 FIN BN
(OPCON FOR			6/501 (GS)		3 TPD (DS		55PSB
MVMT)			BAND (GS)		18 MP Co)		316 Post CO
596 Maint Co			323 MP DET				834 Post Det
(OPCON FOR			CID				1 ASOS(-)
MVMT)							14 PAD
5/D/1-4 ADA (GS)							141 mil history det
SEC/1/B/141 SIG							6 DET /7
(SEN) (DS)							WEATHER

This medium is

UNCLASSIFIED

U.S. Government Property

The 1st Armored Division monument to its fallen on display at the parade ground at Wiesbaden, Germany. On two sides, it displays the names of the 130 soldiers lost in action with the task force. Formally dedicated in July 2005 in a special park next to the command post, it will accompany the division to its new garrison of Ft. Bliss, Texas, in 2007.

The turnovers of the respective 2d brigades and engineer brigades in the center followed. The DIVARTY headquarters and 4th brigades were next in sequence, the former taking responsibility for BIAP, while the 501st Military Intelligence Battalion assumed responsibility for intelligence support to the Baghdad area. The DISCOMs exchanged responsibility for Forward Logistics Base Dogwood (40km/25 miles southwest of BIAP) on May 26.

Gen Sanchez took operational control and responsibility for TF Baghdad units and the area of responsibility as of 0600hrs May 29, 2003. The two 1st brigades transferred authority in their northeastern sector on June 5, completing the realignment of the forces. In only two weeks, the 1st Armored Division had moved over 8,000 vehicles and 15,000 soldiers via tactical road marches, Heavy Equipment Transporters (HETs), and intratheater airlift from the staging camps in Kuwait, and had assumed responsibility for the vital sectors of the Iraqi capital. Gen Sanchez and over 30,000 troops of TF 1st Armored Division had now undertaken the responsibility for all stability operations in the city. The commander also maintained vital connections with and responsibilities to the US occupation authorities, other US and coalition military and government activities, foreign representation such as embassies, as well as V Corps (later designated CJTF 7) and higher headquarters in the theater.

The enemy in many forms

The threats to US forces and their operations remaining after the collapse of Saddam Hussein's regime consisted of isolated pockets of disorganized military resistance, a large criminal element (which heavily infested Baghdad because of their release from prisons on the eve of the war), and emerging subversives or insurrectionist movements. The earliest classification of a post-hostilities threat group was that of

"Former Regime Loyalists" (FRL). These included Ba'ath Party members, former Iraqi soldiers, and remnants of the Fedayeen Saddam (a radical paramilitary group loosely recruited into the Iraqi defense establishment). "Extremist groups" were also classified, to include Wahabi Islamic extremists, the Iraqi Islamic Party, and various pro-regime tribes. The extremist groups could be augmented by outside groups, including international terrorists interested in exploiting the unrest and possible US vulnerabilities.

The FRL continued efforts to reorganize under various groupings in order to force the withdrawal of coalition forces and regain power within Iraq. They operated among several cities within the Sunni Triangle from Ar Ramadi in the west to Baghdad in the east, and north to Mosul. The largest group connected to activity in Baghdad was "Mohammad's Army."

FRL forces were well armed. Although initially poorly trained, they proved capable of lethal attacks against the coalition forces and Iraqis who sided with them. The intelligence services considered the FRL forces as compatible with other groups, such as foreign fighters, transnational terrorist elements, pro-Saddam tribes, radical Kurdish factions, and Islamic extremist elements throughout Iraq. FRL elements continuously attempted to gain favor in militant Sunni neighborhoods throughout Baghdad. They all used private homes to conduct meetings and cache their weapons. During the period of its occupation of Baghdad, the 1st Armored Division considered Ba'athist leadership cadres and the FRL as the primary threats to coalition operations. They probably were responsible for the majority of ambushes against soft targets such as convoys and symbolic centers of the interim government such as police stations and council meeting locations.

Sunni extremists attempted to force the coalition's withdrawal in order to establish a religious fundamentalist state. Their operating area conformed largely to the Sunni Triangle. However, the concentration of Sunni extremists within the 1st Armored Division zone of operations appeared to be the southern and western portions of Baghdad and in sectors further west toward al-Fallujah. These groups reportedly consorted with foreign fighters crossing the Syrian borders to areas within Iraq.

The Supreme Council for the Islamic Revolution in Iraq (SCIRI; a Shi'ite political party and armed militia) took advantage of the security vacuum to increase its presence and influence throughout Iraq. SCIRI's goal of a non-secular but independent state run by Iraqis probably reduced their traditional support from Iran, however. In addition, the collapse of the Ba'athist regime advanced the relative influence of Ayatollah Sistani and other important clerics of the key Shi'ite holy cities of an Najaf and Karbala throughout Iraq. The renewed emphasis on an Najaf as a

An engineer of TF Baghdad stands by his duty position, operating a generator, likely in an FOB; his rifle is ready, PASGT body armor and helmet are worn, magazines filled, water and rations at his side, including a voltmeter. This posture symbolizes the dedication to duty of the soldiers of TF Baghdad in 2003–04: ready for the challenge yet also a bit weary and bored and willing to indulge in a good read – a novel, the Bible, perhaps even a service or technical handbook. Combat, as in most wars, came in fleeting and unexpected moments, punctuating an unrelenting boredom that required the human spirit to overcome it. Suffice to say that US soldiers of 2003–04 proved equal to the task, and more.

Street looters apprehended by soldiers. By September 2003, the revived Iraqi police and other security elements began to have an effect upon street crime in Baghdad, releasing more soldiers for combat tasks.

center of the Shi'a religion countered the former influence of Iranian clerics seeking to fill the void, thus causing undoubted friction between Shi'ite elements.

The Badr Corps, the military arm of SCIRI, retained much stronger ties to Tehran and it continued open anti-coalition demonstrations. The Badr Corps followers in Iran reportedly crossed into Iraq with Iranian intelligence agents within their organization. They were considered likely to have placed arms stockpiles in the Shi'a sections of Baghdad, and other cities to the south. SCIRI later changed the name of its militia to the Badr Organization, suggesting a more peaceful and political emphasis, but it remained a significant military presence in Iraqi public life.

Religious organizations, while not directly rising against US and coalition forces, remained vital sources of support for the insurrection and other forms of opposition to them. The Howza (religious seminaries teaching Islamic theory and law once banned under Saddam) provided three key structures for the Shi'a: the premier religious school in the Shi'a religion located in an Najaf; a body of leaders that guided the direction and conduct of the Shi'a religion; and the mutually shared goals of all Shi'as. All Shi'a-based organizations opposing the coalition forces had some affiliation with the Howza, including SCIRI, the Badr Corps, and the Iranian Dawa Party. Several persons claimed to speak on behalf of the Howza, such as the influential religious leader Muqtada al-Sadr, son of a murdered Shi'ite cleric, and Ayatollah Sistani.

Wahabists are a Saudi Arabian-oriented, radical religious organization that preaches non-tolerance of infidels, jihad against coalition forces, and martyrdom in the name of these goals. The focus of Wahabist influence remained with the Sunni tribes in the vicinity of al-Fallujah with some support among their co-religionists within Baghdad. Baghdad Sunni and Ba'ath Party members typically remained more secular in thought than Wahabists, but they would occasionally cooperate as a matter of convenience. US and coalition forces identified elements of several recognized terrorist organizations in Iraq and these groups may have received support from the FRL. Some of the Islamic extremist organizations suspected in the enemy ranks included al-Qaeda, Ansar al-Islam, Hizbollah, and Wahabi extremists.

Criminals remained a large, destabilizing influence in Baghdad, and their activities undermined the goal of the United States and its allies to quickly restore and stabilize civil life in the capital and country. Randomly executed violent crimes continued throughout Baghdad in mid-2003, such as murder, kidnapping, assault, rape, theft, looting, and carjacking. Abandoned industrial and warehouse areas often contained weapons caches and arms markets. The black market continued to be the center of illicit activity and the primary trading site for looted items. The stolen items included power generators and the copper from stolen cables, the theft of which sharply curtailed the restoration of utility services within Baghdad. Black marketeers sold weapons throughout the city and supplied paramilitary organizations of all kinds. Other illicit activities, such as prostitution and extortion rings, threatened the security within Baghdad and undermined public faith that the United States could restore or maintain order within the city.

In order to execute the Relief in Place (RIP) with the 3d Infantry Division and maintain security and stabilization, leaders and troops at all levels had carried out essential orientation exercises and operations in tandem with their counterparts. Old Ironsides first patrolled alongside and assisted 3d Infantry Division in their patrols, then gradually, on mutual agreement, assumed responsibility for operations, ensuring a smooth transition of forces. Before this happened, the incoming 1st Armored Division units took over security of all vital infrastructure and institutions in their assigned sectors, introduced themselves to local leaders, as well as leaders of coalition authority and non-governmental organizations (NGOs), took over supervision of local infrastructure projects, and assumed responsibilities for equipment and supplies. They also continued the process of collecting and disposing of Unexploded Ordnance (UXO), weapons, and munitions caches.

Organizing the force

In addition to forming TF 1st Armored Division by adding major units, such as 2d ACR and 2d/82d Airborne Division, the division commander

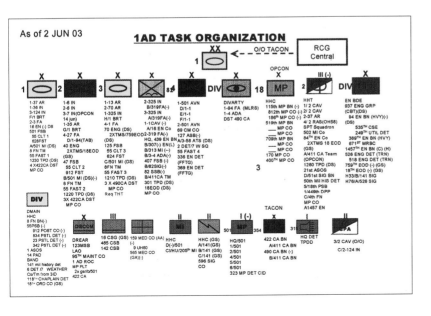

The enlarged task organization for the Baghdad occupation and security mission added combat power in the form of 2d/82d Airborne Division and 2d ACR; MP and civil affairs units each swelled to brigade size and the engineer component became even larger.

ordered an extensive task organization to bring a proper combat balance across the major commands. Accordingly, the normally armor-heavy 1st and 3d brigades received infantry battalions, respectively the 3/124th Infantry from the Florida Army National Guard 53d Infantry Brigade and 1/325th Parachute Infantry cross-attached from the 2d/82d. The 2d/82d in turn received ground troops from the divisional cavalry squadron for increased armor and mobility. The 1st Brigade gave up 2/37th Armor to furnish armored power to the 2d ACR, which had converted to the wheeled "light cavalry regiment" organization and no longer had organic tanks. Conversely, the 2d ACR attached its 3d Squadron to 2d Brigade, providing more infantry and wheeled mobility to the crucial task of guarding the "Green Zone" in central Baghdad. Later in the campaign, the 2/504th Parachute Infantry was attached to the DIVARTY (functioning here as the DCT) as reinforcement for the BIAP security mission.

Additional reinforcements of military police (MP) and engineer units required for the SOSO mission in Baghdad caused the formation of an enlarged division engineer brigade, built around the 937th Engineer Group, and the assignment of the 18th Military Police Brigade to the operational control of the division commander, who now commanded the equivalent of nine maneuver brigades. Further reinforcements, such as a civil affairs brigade, chemical company, psychological operations companies, aeromedical evacuation detachment, finance and personnel support, and other types of augmentation generally remained under division control for the entire deployment in Baghdad, frequently placing detachments with the BCTs. At one time or another, 14 brigade headquarters operated under the control of TF 1st Armored Division.

In this manner, TF 1st Armored Division established five balanced BCTs in Baghdad, each equipped with necessary protection and support. Integral logistics support was provided by their forward support battalions. The adjacent BIAP area was garrisoned by division combat support units, and it furnished ideal command and control facilities, plus an airbase for divisional and air cavalry aviation to support the task force at large. As rehearsed in the urban warfare seminars of February and March, the units occupied a large number of FOBs, which were closed or consolidated and upgraded to support the soldiers as they went to work on a damaged and unsettled city.

The Baghdad mission

Although the planning for the invasion of Iraq was over a year in gestation, precious little planning for Phase IVB (post-hostilities) existed by the time TF 1st Armored Division took up its responsibilities. Instead, most authorities high in the US government presumed that the Iraqis would replace the cupola of its government with new leaders, and an intact government, police, and services bureaucracy would return to work and assist immediately in the recovery effort. However, once the dust had settled from the combat phase, US and coalition forces saw a gravely deteriorated polity and infrastructure. The forces in theater had focused upon the offensive scenarios as they conducted the Iraq campaign. On orders of higher commands, they left the military government and reconstruction efforts to other organizations that presumably would be tasked for this effort once combat had concluded. The rapid termination

Baghdad presented all the problematic types of urban military terrain one could imagine. Traffic coursed through wide boulevards to narrow alleys, separating government and high-rise buildings. There were packed residential areas, industrial parks, underground bunkers and passageways, rivers, lakes, and parks, but all in various stages of decay or damage resulting from decades of conflict and embargo.

of formal combat left only the combat forces on the scene. Thus, the occupiers of Iraq in April 2003 faced several harsh realities.

Despite the US forces' efforts to minimize damage to the city, most public services collapsed as a result of the combat operations, the flight of civil service and other public workers, and the concomitant wholescale looting of buildings and infrastructure. There was no rapid restoration of services on the part of the Iraqis, and the US military forces had neither the expertise nor materiel to begin much-needed reconstruction of the Iraqi infrastructure. The "rolling start" strategic method of the 2003 campaign minimized the employment of forces of all kinds. An eventual build-up of forces was planned, in the event that Iraqi resistance continued or setbacks to the offensive caused new operations to be launched. However, the rapid movement of the initial assault forces brought the "decapitation" of the Saddam Hussein regime in a mere 16 days, leaving the same assault forces now in charge of a large and unplanned stabilization operation. In fact, a nation-building program far in excess of that conducted in the 1990s by NATO in the Balkans now beckoned the United States and its coalition partners. But the assault forces stood alone, recovering from their own exertions, and the follow-on forces scheduled to conduct the remainder of the fighting expected in Iraq, such as 1st Armored Division, were still arriving and assembling.

A great improvisation now took place – a rolling occupation plan, matching the "rolling start" campaign plan. Gen Sanchez later remarked:

> When we arrived in Baghdad, everything was gone. There was no police force, no government. There were no schools. We had to build across military, diplomatic, information and economic lines. We provided direct support to Ambassador Paul Bremmer, then the chief administrator in Iraq, through Central Command. Our soldiers were put into a situation where they had to handle missions across all aspects of Iraqi society … fielding a really flexible, applicable force that was not afraid to take risks or engage in all these different areas, to the point where they achieved remarkable successes. The fact that Iraq was able to move forward in terms of its economy, its entire political infrastructure, with the

The badly damaged and deteriorated city services posed immediate problems for an occupying force trying to provide security, but also attempting to win over the population by demonstrating its power to restore normalcy. The sewage collection and treatment system was the most resistant to reconstruction.

establishment of city councils and national governments – due largely to soldiers on the ground – is phenomenal. Bremmer issued a policy directive that our force was to go out there and make [positive things] happen. Then, we just wanted to help the people, giving them an idea of what freedom means and what democracy is all about – what it means to truly respect human rights, and what strength of diversity is. All of that was exemplified by our soldiers on the ground and in their daily interactions with the people of Iraq.

Sanchez and TF 1st Armored Division now entered into a world of uncertainty. In a planning vacuum, the commander and his staff worked to devise a campaign plan, gather essential intelligence for the mission and tasks, and orchestrate the combat and civil affairs tactics, techniques, and procedures that would best accomplish the coalition objectives. The V Corps headquarters converted to Joint Task Force Seven and now exercised command and control over a multinational force drawing contingents and representatives from over 30 countries. Its responsibilities extended over all Iraq and it reported directly to the new CPA (under Bremmer). This entity was the newly formed occupation authority (the highest US political agency in the country) to oversee the establishment of a new Iraqi government. Somehow, from this constellation of agencies, a new Iraq was supposed to emerge, with reformed political institutions, rebuilt infrastructure, and a re-energized society.

Events would prove the division's first planning effort too optimistic and limited. Assuming a steady improvement in general conditions in Iraq, the initial campaign plan (June 2003) considered that the security situation would see decreased opposition to US forces. The CPA would presumably revive native institutions and governmental bodies at local and national levels. The ongoing US military actions would destroy surviving paramilitary forces, and support for FRLs, such as Ba'athist leaders, would decrease as the latter were captured, tried, or killed. The presumed improvement of basic services and the transfer of Iraqi sovereignty to an interim government would undercut the opposition of radical anti-Western religious groups, as well as the potential violence

Training the new ICDC, later the NIA, became a chief concern for TF 1st Armored Division, and here the 2d Brigade 82d Airborne and 2d ACR took the lead in training troops and leaders in an ICDC Academy system. Here recruits learn combat movement techniques.

between traditionally opposed factions in the country. Above all, it assumed that Iraqi institutions had survived the combat phase, as well as the depredations of the regime in its final years, and were capable of performing their usual functions and security efforts. The end of combat would also bring economic recovery and permit the repair of damaged infrastructure, thus promoting a newly emerging democratic government and discrediting anti-Western factions.

The campaign plan called for the destruction of the remaining paramilitary forces and the installation of Iraqi civil guard forces during July 2003. At the same time, an Iraqi army would begin to form, public services resume their functions, and US military forces could free up manpower for new initiatives. In August these initiatives would include a program of training for the New Iraqi Army (NIA), neutralizing subversives, and defeating remaining criminal gangs. Protecting the first local elections would encourage transitions to local authority, permitting the removal of US forces from urban areas. The division planned to move out of the city to consolidated FOBs in late September and remain ready to conduct combat operations, assist or otherwise reinforce Iraqi

The two architects of the military occupation of Baghdad: MG Ricardo S. Sanchez (left) prepared the 1st Armored Division and led it to Baghdad, where he took responsibility for the security and stabilization of the city and adjoining area. Promoted to lead the military command for all Iraq, he turned the TF Baghdad mission over on July 16, 2003 to BG Martin E. Dempsey (right), a seasoned armor officer already experienced in regional affairs.

BG Dempsey foresaw the year-long deployment cycle of US forces and instituted Rest & Recuperation (R&R) procedures for the command, to include breaks taken in inner city recreation facilities for the "internal furlough" of soldiers, whenever feasible. Here a large swimming facility in the Green Zone serves just such needs.

security forces, and even expand the divisional zone of responsibilities as organizations such as the airborne units and 3d ACR (western Iraq) began to redeploy back to home stations. By early December the 1st Armored Division would leave its FOBs and redeploy to home stations. The "end state" under this plan foresaw the destruction of significant opposition to the Iraqi government. The plan expected that the Iraqis, for their part, would emplace site protection forces and full police capabilities, and establish an interim government with a new army in training. A single US light infantry division would suffice to replace the multi-division occupation force of the previous six months.

The campaign plan emerged over a period of harsh lessons and experiences for the 1st Armored Division, accompanied by major changes in command. MG Sanchez left the division to assume command of V Corps/JTF-7 in the grade of lieutenant general on June 14, and BG Martin E. Dempsey took command on July 16. Dempsey had commanded an armored battalion in the division in the early 1990s, had considerable experience in the armor branch, including command of the 3d ACR, and had directed the key US military missions in Saudi Arabia since August 2001.

After much deliberation, BG Dempsey and his staff published a new campaign plan on August 8. In it, 1st Armored Division stated its mission as *simultaneously* conducting combat operations and SOSO operations, as well as preparing to attack into adjacent sectors in support of tasks ordered by higher headquarters. The combat operations aimed at destroying enemy forces in order to establish a secure civil environment, while the SOSO operations supported the establishment of Iraqi sovereignty.

In addition, the division now planned to undertake – either wholly or in part – the tasks of training and equipping the Iraqi security forces, to include police, civil defense, Facility Protection Services (FPS), and the NIA. A humanitarian assistance program aimed at preventing unnecessary hardship to the population of Baghdad worked in tandem with an effort to assist in restoring essential services to the community. The protection of key sites (water, power, sewage, etc.) also contributed to general security and recovery. The division saw the need to protect its own lines of communication and to synchronize its operations with higher political and military headquarters in Iraq. The huge amount of UXO and cached munitions and arms required clearing throughout the

US Infantrymen, 1st Battalion, 36th Infantry "Spartans," 2004

OLD IRONSIDES

A

B

Close-quarters battle drill, 2d Battalion, 325th Airborne Infantry "White Falcons"

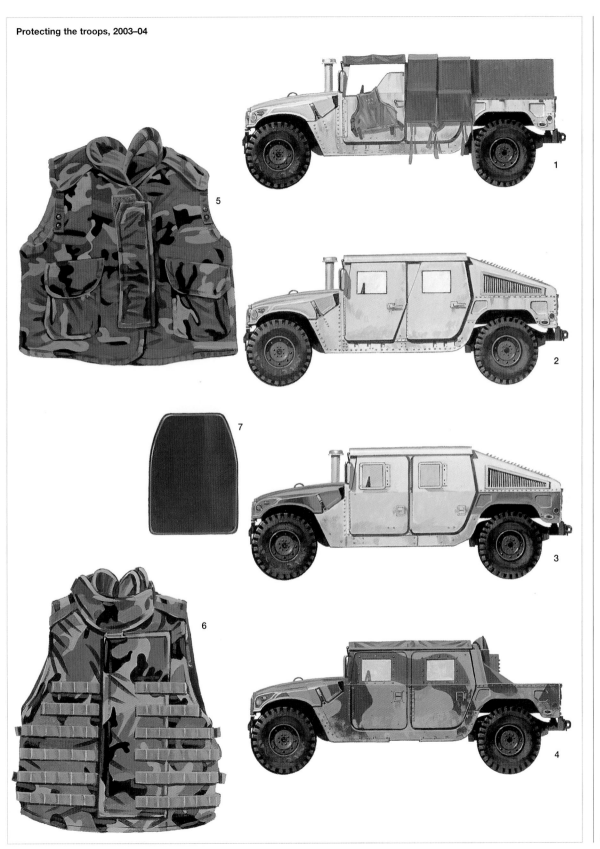

US infantry of 2d Battalion, 6th Infantry "Gators" on raid

D

A Forward Operating Base (FOB), Baghdad, November 2003

E

Combat at Karbala, TF 1st Battalion, 37th Armor "Bandits," May 2004

F

G

zone, and previous efforts had only scratched the surface of the problem. Finally, in recognition of the more lengthy process it had entered into, the division planned to conduct training, maintenance, and personnel (Morale, Welfare, and Recreation – MWR) operations in order to ensure constant readiness for new missions or deployments.

Significant new features of the 1st Armored Division campaign plan included the continuation of combat operations, because the enemy now demonstrated increasing resilience. Maintaining unit readiness and proficiency required a systematic logistics and maintenance effort, as well as construction of an array of field gunnery ranges for all arms. In addition, the recognition that the deployment would now extend up to 12 months led to "environmental leave" and shorter in-theater furloughs for a portion of the force that could be prised away from essential duties to rest and recover.

Instead of eradicating enemy resistance and bringing absolute security to the area of operations, the division now recognized the longer term nature of the struggle and proposed to defeat the FRL forces, neutralize extremist groups, and reduce crime by 50 percent. In order to accomplish this, it would establish, equip, and train a large security force to replace the virtually disappeared security of the city: 16,000 police, four battalions of a new ICDC, and 5,500 FPS guards. A large array of public works projects, funded by a variety of programs, as well as conventional civil affairs programs, would assist in restoring economic life to the city and maintaining an acceptable and sustainable quality of life, especially in the supply of power, fuel, water, and sanitation services. In this regard, the re-opening of BIAP and the introduction of a new currency were considered major benchmarks. Finally, the division undertook the task of assisting at all levels of government in order to install viable and fair neighborhood, district, and city governing councils.

Under a concept that recognized "an adapting enemy," the campaign plan foresaw an opposition capable of changing tactics and targets in order to evade US actions, and one that would adjust to improving local security measures. However, actions against the FRL forces and the reduction of criminal activities to manageable proportions could bear fruit by the beginning of 2004. The objective was that only extremist groups, the most unpredictable, would remain likely opponents by the time of the turnover to the cavalry division. In the process, the most likely enemy actions would come in the form of isolated, random, and individual attacks, with the occasional primitive organized or combined attack. Less likely, but much more dangerous, would be the enemy mounting an organized, well-targeted, and highly lethal attack with massive effects. In addition, the potential for the enemy to disrupt political reconstruction of the country with political assassinations was well recognized.

A city to secure
Each district of Baghdad had unique characteristics for the assigned brigades to deal with, but the tasks the brigades undertook had much in common. Certain high-value facilities, such as public works, oil refineries, nuclear plants, universities, BIAP, and government complexes like the Green Zone, required a considerable force to protect round the clock. The recruiting and preparing of an auxiliary force from the Iraqi

population thus became an early requirement for the 1st Armored Division. This program yielded the FPS, consisting of uniformed and lightly armed security guards who could maintain the required 24-hour guard presence over many of the fixed locations of value. This force could prevent looting, but could not stand up to deliberate attack by the more heavily armed threat groups. However, with proper communications equipment, training, supervision, and increasing experience, and US forces nearby or in support, the guards began to provide the beginnings of a local security base. In the same vein, the recovering civilian police benefited from the nearby positions and patrols of the TF 1st Armored Division and, with assured support, they began to demonstrate improved capabilities.

The increasing availability of Iraqi security manpower eased the burden on the task of providing physical protection for an impossible number of sites in this city of over 5 million inhabitants. These two soldiers on guard, armed with M16A2 rifles, are probably not drawn from the combat arms units of the division.

In addition to fixed positions, soldiers provided mobile patrols as the main streets and designated military support routes of the city required surveillance and periodic patrolling to prevent ambushes and maintain the freedom of movement for security forces throughout the city. As the campaign developed and the use of Improvised Explosive Devices (IEDs) by the enemy increased, the patrols became essential to the early discovery and neutralization of these weapons, even though they were among the prime targets of the IED tactics. What soldiers soon found was that only a very aggressive and energetic patrolling effort kept the routes reasonably clear. Repeated experiences taught the soldiers how to spot unusual and suspicious objects and increasing knowledge of the tactics and techniques of IED employment gradually reduced their effectiveness in the districts. The use of VBIED complicated the patrolling and fixed surveillance tactics, because they were very large, blended well into civilian traffic, and could be used with little warning in suicide attacks.

Aerial patrols came in the form of sorties of OH-58D scout and UH-60 utility helicopters of the division's 4th Brigade, operating 15 and 16 respectively, as well as the air cavalry squadron of the 2d ACR (21 and 8, respectively). These flew day-and-night route and area reconnaissance missions in support of the task force. In the event of opposition, they could call upon the fire support of the brigade covering the district, or backup from the 4th Brigade's 18 AH-64 attack helicopters, at least two of which stood on ready alert status at all times at BIAP. During 15 months of continuous combat operations, the "Iron Eagles" flew over

The aviation component of the task force consisted of 4th Brigade squadrons, here on the BIAP flight line, and the air cavalry squadron of 2d ACR, at Redcatcher Airfield. Note AH-64A Apache gunships in the foreground and OH-58D Kiowa scouts to the rear.

39,000 hours while supporting a total of 6,747 missions, consumed 3,826,000 gallons (14,481,410 liters) of fuel, and performed countless hours of maintenance in some of the harshest desert conditions.

While 4th Brigade aviation operated out of BIAP, the 2d ACR helicopters remained autonomous at their Redcatcher Field site adjacent to FOB Muleskinner in southeast Baghdad. Such dispersion also enabled aviation support even if one facility came under attack. BIAP had multiple users in any case. Special operations units based aircraft there and the air forces of coalition forces, some civilian cargo planes, and airliners made frequent stops, completing the array of traffic. An ad hoc airfield management team was formed to operate the facility, consisting of the 4th Brigade air control and safety sections, various US Air Force teams, Australian air traffic controllers, civilian contractors, and a local national airport manager. Later in the campaign, the 4th Brigade received the additional mission of BIAP ground defense, including districts immediately surrounding the airport, and also took responsibility for countering the missiles, mortars, and rockets launched against local aircraft and the airport. This was a considerable mission load for an aviation brigade staff, and its augmentation became necessary. These additions included additional operations' watch officers to monitor the ground situation and specialists to assist in planning defensive measures, patrolling, reaction forces, rules of engagement, and a plethora of matters not usually undertaken by an aviation unit.

The 1st Armored Division frequently provided escorts for convoys of troops, supplies, and VIPs traveling over the city's thoroughfares. The helicopter resources also participated in these efforts, and enhanced the freedom of movement that the division usually enjoyed. On the ground, the tanks and BFVs saw considerable use, but the battalions of armor and mechanized infantry received extra "Humvee" utility vehicles to augment their fighting vehicles and to enable the same crews to participate in patrol or escort missions where their heavier vehicles remained too large or just unnecessary for the task at hand. The "hardness" of the Humvee vehicles remained a critical issue for all US troops, including the Iron Soldiers, through the deployment, as three different levels of protection

Of the thousands of Humvee utility vehicles taken into Iraq in 2003, only a handful, the designated weapons carriers for MP, antitank and scout units, featured protective armor as shown in this photo of an MP patrol. Belatedly, a program to armor all of these vehicles began and a few hundred came into the hands of the task force before it departed.

appeared in the "up-armored" vehicles and only one offered adequate protection against the IEDs being employed by the enemy. As a result, units procured locally fabricated steel plates to augment the scant protection of otherwise unarmored HMMWVs (see Plate C).

In accordance with 1st Armored Division's plans, Iraqi security forces came on line under the task force's protection, freeing the division for the planning and execution of offensives from the FOBs against targeted opposition groups. The objective for this part of the campaign was the literal control of the streets of Baghdad, first against the criminal gangs, but increasingly against the FRL elements, which were entering the city from their rallying points in the Sunni Triangle, al-Fallujah, and the sparsely garrisoned zone south of the capital.

In this unofficial battle of Baghdad, the key use of targeting boards or committees, on the part of both division and brigades, served to best apply the slender thread of manpower that could be spared from the security effort for offensive actions. The targeting boards brought together the staffs of combat units, supporting arms, intelligence, civil affairs, information operations, psychological operations, and other government agencies as required. They reviewed reports on a daily basis to form a common picture of the enemy known to be operating in each district and forwarded proposals for actions to the division targeting board for assessment and consolidation. In this way, the initiative of the brigades was maintained and the division commander was able to allocate his resources best by sequencing the brigade efforts. As the campaign progressed, the emphasis increasingly went to the lower level commanders' estimates and initiatives, given their wider access to local sources of intelligence via informers and other methods. Each battalion and company commander held responsibility for his "neighborhoods," including not just their security, but also installing local government, schools, and public works, and spurring on business or economic recovery. Accordingly, junior officers would meet regularly with local leaders of municipalities, mosques, and police to air grievances and spread US support for local inhabitants, using organic construction efforts as well as US funds for contracting services.

On the south side of Redcatcher FOB of the 2d ACR, this abandoned building in the old Iraqi military academy grounds later became useful for the basic training of the ICDC. Both 2d ACR and 2d/82d Airborne operated the ICDC academy courses that produced the first ready brigade of that organization and the future Iraqi army. These damaged structures had to serve as the initial garrison facilities for the US forces in Baghdad, through that hot, miserable summer of 2003, before reconstruction efforts could produce first temporary, and, later, enduring FOB facilities.

With this strategy in mind, the division's policy of sending interpreters and other observers to the local mosques to listen to the Friday orations and review the leaflets and other indicators of ambience was useful. The observations correlated well with the activities of the opposition groups in a given district or neighborhood. Moreover, local leaders who queried US military leaders over unit actions could be encouraged to talk to their imams and the population at large about the attitudes toward the coalition forces and how the conduct of individuals improved or detracted from local security and quality of life.

As an example, some of the first reports taken by the division (which are recorded here verbatim) showed a considerable variety of sentiments in the local population:

CPT L_____ had his interpreter record what was being said from the loud speakers of the local Mosque at [location]. The following is the gist of what the translator could discern:

- The US Army conquered Iraq by making a deal with Arab leaders.
- We must ask all Arab Nations to fight against the US Army, we must not be silent and ask the Iraqi people to fight the US Army.
- We couldn't stop the US Army because of disunity between Arab nations.
- There was an American who visited the Ministry of Religion and he said that this Ministry must lead by Sunni, Shiite and Christian. That is a bad thought because this ministry leads by Sunni only. All that this ministry has belongs to all Sunni.
- The Iran Government sent some people to the gate of one of our Mosques and they tried to lead Al Shiite from it because Al-Shiite in Iran tried to have unity with Sunni.
- We must have Shiite and Al-Sunni to have unity to fight US Army and fight and bring with them all what they want to Iraq.

And from other districts:

Results of Friday sermons:
- [Unit] reports collection on mosques in zones 25, 26, 39 and 41 from 1100–2130.
- Mosques reportedly used pre recorded prayer calls and there was no anti-us sentiment.
- Mosques had approximately 200 pax. in attendance and environment was reported as non-threatening and docile compared to other Fridays.
- [Unit translators] report they went to one mosque – Al M_____ and report that there were leaflets passed (had no copy of the leaflets) stating that the people of Iraq should not wait for god to kill "the enemy" and to shoot every inch of their

bodies. They did not report the originator of the leaflets;

- [Unit] report they went to Al S____ mosque, zone ___. Mosque was filled to only ~80% capacity. Report stated attendees were late in arriving, and no anti-coalition or political remarks were made. The atmosphere was calm and relaxed.

Because the SOSO mission was going to leave the division critically short of infantry, the artillery battalions converted to this role, leaving only a few gun platoons ready for fire support missions in the division zone. To the everlasting credit of

the artillerymen, they accomplished this conversion virtually unassisted. Drawing upon internal expertise, they retrained and deployed into all the same tasks as did their infantry and mechanized infantry brethren. These included the DS battalions of the brigades and the 2d ACR, as well as the general support battalion (equipped with Multiple Launch Rocket Systems – MLRS) under the control of DIVARTY, the 1/94th Field Artillery, which provided most of the infantry "muscle" for the BIAP force under the DIVARTY commander. The few fire missions handled in the division zone were provided by howitzer platoons kept ready in the 2/319th (2d/82d Airborne Division), 4/27th, and 2/3d Field Artillery battalions.

Tank crewmen in the armor battalions had to adapt to infantry roles but also remain ready to mount their M1A1 tanks and add armored firepower to any mission or task on order. When the tank was not required, they patrolled in Humvees or operated dismounted as infantrymen.

Engineers, of course, carry a secondary mission to operate as infantry, but it should be noted that all the soldiers of TF 1st Armored Division pulled their share of the burdens of patrolling, manning TCPs and other checkpoints, FOB guard duty, and even filling in on offensive missions such as raids and neighborhood sweeps. Because of the shortage of female soldiers to search female civilians and suspects, nearly every female soldier in the task force eventually served in such assignments. The army tradition of "every soldier a rifleman" proved well grounded in the Baghdad campaign, to nobody's surprise.

One brigade commander, Peter Mansoor, summarized the effort:

We assigned missions based on who owned a zone. All my land owners had similar capabilities for routine patrols and raids. The difference came in assigning reserve responsibilities. I usually had an armor or mech company/team on REDCON 3 status (move in 30 minutes) and a second one on REDCON 4 status (move in 60 minutes). These came out of TF 1-36 IN and TF 1-37 AR, but were usually used in 2-3 FA's zone (Adhamiya), which was the hot spot in the Brigade's area of operations. I normally didn't have a hot arty platoon, but rather usually used mortars as the counter fire weapon of choice. We had mortars on a 24/7 hot gun status, capable of firing within 1 minute of notice. "Operation Whitetail"

OPPOSITE AND ABOVE **This pair of photos illustrates the searching of Iraqi homes that became necessary for the security mission. Opposite, an Iraqi ICDC soldier, teamed with a task force search team is looking into a doorway. Note the improvised armor shield. Their weapons were issued from captured Iraqi army stocks. Above, 1st Armored Division soldiers look through documents and other material during a search. They wear full protective gear, to which pistols, flashlights, and a night-vision scope are hung for easy use.**

At a TCP, a soldier uses a conventional electronic metal detector to search civilians. He wears his M16A2 rifle slung in front, with an M9 pistol equally available in a shoulder holster. Although his OTV has a SAPI plate, he eschews the throat and side protectors, probably because of the searing heat of the day.

IED clearance patrols used armored vehicles (Bradleys, tanks, uparmored HMMWVs) along with Warlock jammers to search for IEDs.

The BIAP sector proved especially burdensome for the division, because of its obvious value as a prestige target and, on the contrary, a symbolic coalition success in the event that it could be returned to "normal" operations. The US Federal Aviation Administration exercised authority over the restoration of the airport for operations, but the division remained responsible for its defense. The presence of many civilian agencies, sections of the CPA, CJTF-7/V Corps headquarters, and the flow of visitors and logistics through the airport, once it began restricted operations, greatly complicated the defensive measures. The airport access soon devolved upon contracted services of the US government, and the DIVARTY commander concentrated on exterior defense matters, becoming much less of a military mayor of the district than was the case with the commanders in the other districts. The perimeter was manned and active mobile patrolling covered the approaches and maintained observation over danger zones. The 1/4th Air Defense Artillery Battalion proved highly useful with its Avengers (Humvees mounted with two Stinger launchers) and Bradley Stinger Fighting Vehicles (BSFV), providing both firepower and good day/night surveillance capabilities. Both the battalions under the DCT remained very active, covering the airport perimeter and the adjacent neighborhoods of the district until relieved by the 4th Brigade in January 2004.

The BIAP also became a magnet for mortar and artillery rocket fire from the insurgent forces. However, damaging the airport with random attacks proved to be an illusion, because of its expanse. The tactics of the DIVARTY units in maintaining observation on likely firing sites, tracking attacks visually and with counter-battery radars (TPQ-36/37), and aggressive patrolling proved effective counters to the attacks. In addition, the BIAP district had to contend with the threat of hand-held antiaircraft missiles (known as Man-Portable Air Defense Systems – MANPADS) directed against air traffic.

Stability operations

An enduring characteristic of the SOSO campaign in Iraq was the seemingly inexhaustible supply of insurgent weapons and munitions. The regime had accumulated massive supplies of materiel through its several wars fought against neighboring countries and the West since the early 1980s. The rapid collapse of Iraqi resistance in the 2003 campaign left mountains of it unguarded and open to pilferage by all manner of civilians, many of whom armed themselves provisionally in the event of civil war breaking out or just to guard against or threaten their local rivals. Finding arms and munitions caches became a daily experience for the soldiers, as well as UXO fired by each side in the combat phase of the campaign. The 1st Armored Division launched Operation *Clean Sweep* to locate and secure caches and *Iron Bullet* to convey them to disposal sites, but in the event, these functions became permanent and there was never a pause in the discovery, securing, and clearing of these lethal resources. By September 8, 2003, after barely three months in action, TF 1st Armored Division had cleared 2,044 unexploded munitions and 1,927 arms/munitions caches, with 39 and 130 yet to be cleared. Only near the end of its stay in Baghdad did these numbers dwindle (most UXO was cleared in this initial operation) but the later division campaign south of Baghdad found more mountains of ordnance to be secured. The size of the caches in the city ranged from less than a single truckload to bulky items like antiaircraft and artillery missiles, requiring cranes and flatbed trailers to remove.

Civil affairs teams spread out in the assigned districts each day to meet with locals and assess and prioritize the projects that 1st Armored Division could best undertake in the shortest amount of time to improve the Iraqi living conditions. The Commander's Emergency Response

Above all, BIAP remained a major prize of the occupation. Its reopening to civilian traffic would indicate a return to normalcy. Therefore it became a prime target for the insurgents who attempted numerous bombardments and tried to bring down aircraft with MANPADS missiles. In the foreground is a chemical biological monitoring site with attendant M93A1 Fox vehicle; behind it is a C-17 transport of the US Air Force.

Program (CERP) proved one of the most effective schemes, as it provided funds to local coalition commanders to let contracts with locals or hire them directly to perform needed tasks in the neighborhoods. Just as recovery was gaining momentum, the CERP funds sequestered from the fallen regime began to run out, which proved most frustrating to the soldiers, who watched contracts get canceled, and left Iraqis idle. In the course of TF 1st Armored Division's mission in Baghdad (as of April 10, 2004) over $65 million was received and $45.5 million allocated to 3,994 deserving projects, 3,713 of which stood complete as of April 10, 2004.

Each local commander administrated CERP, thus enhancing his authority and standing among the civic leaders, who also benefited from cooperating with the coalition program. In place of a bureaucratic process, the program allowed immediate contracting or payment for services, construction, and purchase of goods and materials. The intention was to supplement the larger, more formal, and expensive projects, such as infrastructure overhaul, with timely, low-cost, and high-impact projects. For example, CERP funds allowed the construction of 88 neighborhood advisory council buildings in Baghdad, which never existed under the former regime. Throughout Iraq, 991 CERP projects specifically supported these newly established local governments, as well as Iraq's legal system. For the first time in 30 years, an independent judiciary began functioning, and nearly all of Iraq's 400 courts opened within the first year of occupation.

With the help of CERP funds, all hospitals and clinics reopened, and the neglected health care facilities received a thorough rehabilitation and reconstruction. CERP-funded health projects and pharmaceutical distribution increased 17 times in the first eight months' effort. CERP funds rehabilitated schools, most of which opened in time for the fall 2003 term, with revised textbooks (which had Ba'athist propaganda removed) also purchased under the same program. All universities and technical institutes opened in the first half-year of coalition occupation.

The seemingly endless array of munitions left astray or in hidden caches around the country demanded constant vigilance and recovery efforts to safeguard civilians and coalition troops alike. Here antiaircraft missiles, some in storage containers, have been brought to the divisional collection point for eventual destruction.

CERP funds also provided for new police and security force stations and facilities. They allowed early contracting for emergency water and sewer repairs and projects that had collapsed in Baghdad because of looting and neglect.

As the summer set in, water, sewage, and electricity became the new measure of effectiveness in Iraq, and especially Baghdad, which had enjoyed in many of its districts a privileged status in the priority of services. Sadly, the declining infrastructure could not support immediate restoration of services, and the soldiers had to pitch in with major improvisations to assist the population (for instance the division's use of 3d Brigade's cavalry troop to deliver liquefied natural gas to all the districts). On July 5, as temperatures climbed above 114°F (46°C), only one battalion in the division reported as many as 17 hours of electricity in the day, the other 19 units reporting one to ten hours of service. Water supply performed better that day, with two battalions reporting 21 or more hours, 12 others at least 17 hours of water, and the other six reporting one to 15 hours of water. Because of defects in the power grid and other infrastructure problems, the *best* average that Baghdad residents could look forward to by the early fall was a cycle of four hours on and an equal amount off. The US forces, of course, remained well supplied in all commodities within their FOBs.

The three wastewater treatment plants that served Baghdad (Rustimaya North and South, and Karkh), with a total capacity of 204 million gallons (775 million liters) per day, all stood inoperable at the fall of Baghdad. All the waste was running directly into the Tigris River, except for quantities remaining above ground in the streets of some dilapidated neighborhoods.

Engineer units under the direction of the division engineer or engineer brigade commander toiled daily, clearing rubble, removing UXO, repairing damaged or unsafe buildings to keep them functional, improving the FOBs and headquarters sites of the division and CJTF-7, removing obstacles on routes, clearing fields of fire around high-value defended areas, such as BIAP or power plants, providing power generators, and improving distribution in military sites. The subterranean layout of Baghdad not only related to city services, but also to the many government and military underground bunkers, and special facilities with their hidden entrances and connecting tunnels, all of which required reconnaissance, clearing, and some form of security action to prevent their use by insurgents or criminal elements.

Frequently, the military engineers performed well beyond their notional capabilities in the city. Repairing the damaged 14th of July suspension bridge required the design and fabrication of guides and clamps to replace or reinforce frayed cables, a talent supplied by an Army Reserve sergeant first class. Restoring the power supply and climate control system of the BIAP buildings necessary for constant command use required skills brought in by reservists from their civilian trades.

The pace for soldiers in Baghdad never let up from the moment they took charge. In the first month of operations they conducted:

- 24,255 military patrols; 943 joint patrols with Iraqi police.
- 61 offensive missions, to include raids and cordon-and-searches.
- confiscations of 639 AK-47 rifles, 171 rocket launchers, 217 pistols.

Two soldiers of the 1st Armored Division check their mission orders while securing and observing Iraqi workers beginning restoration work on an abandoned building. They wear Interceptor body armor with SAPI, the man on the left adding the groin protector, also wearing the older, strap-on helmet scope mount. Both carry their M4 carbines slung at the ready, with M9 pistols in shoulder holsters. The sergeant first class (right) also wears a grenade pouch attached to his vest, but the lack of attachments to the M4s and other combat gear suggest that combat is not imminent and they may be on rear-echelon duty.

As a result of these combat operations, five soldiers lost their lives and 18 were WIA.

Meanwhile, the division's civil affairs projects already began to make their mark on the city. "Task Force Neighborhood" conducted 18 projects in 14 different zones, repairing 44 schools and 15 police stations, completing 41 major trash removals and other general engineering projects, and refurbishing 22 football (soccer) fields for the communities. The brigades contributed several more such projects as local initiatives, to include repairing six market areas, 30 schools, and renovating high-value and high-visibility facilities such as the al-Rasheed Ministry of Education Building, the Olympic Stadium, and an irrigation system, as well as emplacing a bridge over the Tigris River to replace a span demolished by the Iraqi army during the previous combat operations.

"TF Bullet" removed 2,074 Heavy Expanded Mobile Tactical Truck (HEMTT) loads of UXO, arms, and ammunition, totaling 9,541 short tons (8,654 tonnes). Division engineers removed 1,113 UXOs, marking 79 remaining, and removed 1,265 caches of arms and weapons, with 196 remaining under guard. In total, TF 1st Armored Division had removed over 55 million rounds of small-arms ammunition and over 1 million items of UXO and arms, including the following items of great value to maintaining order:

- 16,620 rifles and pistols.
- 465 machine guns.
- 1,935 rocket launchers (mostly RPGs).
- 186,483 grenades.
- 28,634 artillery rounds.
- 140,484 RPG rounds.

The pace of patrolling activity varied throughout the first year, depending upon weather, other operations, and the assessed enemy situation. A few random examples suffice to indicate the level of daily activity the task force maintained:

Date	Jun 3, '03	Jun 9, '03	Jun 27, '03	Jul 20, '03	Aug 27, '03	Sept 12, '03	Oct 8, '03	Nov 13, '03
Day patrols mounted/dismounted	293/119	433/194	457/181	443/116	240/47	227/45	250/57	261/53
Night patrols mounted/dismounted	265/103	282/142	271/137	235/80	153/51	115/41	150/50	129/49
Raids	1	3	1	8	9	1	1	1
Aviation patrols	11	24	12	11	11		11	12
Arrests or detentions	59	175	248	45	32	27	4	1

June 23–24, 2003 saw the most active 24-hour period for the task force in the early stage of the deployment. Soldiers had to contend with nine small-arms attacks, three grenade incidents, five attacks with rocket launchers (RPG weapons), a possible MANPADS launch, and civilian incidents including one hostage taking, a traffic accident, and an unspecified explosion. None of these were related and the distinction between criminal gangs and FRL remained blurred. As typical temperatures continued to climb above 110°F (43°C), the incident levels did not improve. Frequent reports indicated that the populace sensed that the electricity situation was worsening. The promised power delivery rate of three hours on and three hours off was not being attained. One neighborhood reported not receiving power for seven days. Rumors abounded: that people were being punished for attacks on US forces; that former Ba'ath Party members were running the power plants and turning off the power as revenge for ousting them from their positions; that if you wanted to have power, you must bribe the electrical workers.

The missions continued apace for the soldiers. Some typical examples included raids on July 28 by 1/36th Infantry in an eight-block area to prevent future IED attacks. They searched 149 buildings, detaining 20 individuals and seizing several weapons: 12 AK-47s, six grenades, three 9mm pistols, one 12-ga. shotgun, 26 7.62mm magazines, nine 9mm magazines, 890 rounds of 7.62mm ammunition, 74 rounds of 9mm ammunition, seven protective masks, three small boxes of US currency, three Republican Guard uniforms, 11 passports (four Egyptian), two bayonets, and 1 million Iraqi Dinar. In a separate incident, an Iraqi male tried to run a TCP by attempting to hit two soldiers with his car. The TCP opened fire and killed the Iraqi. A search of his car found no contraband. Two US soldiers were lightly injured when they jumped out of the path of the car, with one receiving scratches to his left shoulder and leg and the other a cut on his hand. Both were treated and returned to the scene.

A day later, a 2/3d Artillery TCP came under fire from the rooftops by two or more gunmen, after all the lights in the neighborhood went out and a red flare was fired into the air. A four-door sedan then approached the TCP at a high rate of speed. When it became apparent that the vehicle would not stop, the soldiers opened fire on the vehicle with M16s and disabled it. Three Iraqi males were in the vehicle: one was severely wounded with gunshot wounds to the head, chest, and arms, and was evacuated to a local civilian hospital. The other two Iraqi occupants were unharmed and detained. A search of the vehicle found no weapons. No US soldiers were injured, but their M998 vehicle had five bullet holes through the windshield.

These two photos show an early danger presented to the soldiers: an improvised multiple rocket launcher. Hidden inside a generator chassis, it contained 40 tubes for 107mm or 81mm rockets, fired electrically from a timer or remote trigger device.

On August 3, a patrol from 16th Engineer Battalion discovered two 82mm mortar tubes with base plates. The equipment was recovered to the battalion operations center. The same day, C Battery, 2/3d Artillery discovered a suspicious box lying along the roadway on a bridge overpass. Explosive Ordnance Disposal (EOD) disabled and recovered the IED. While in the area, EOD noticed two 60mm mortars (with base plates) and three 60mm rounds set up alongside the road. The equipment and ammunition were recovered to the headquarters of 1st Brigade.

These scenes and activities had already become commonplace in a city literally teeming with people and weaponry. The regrettable deaths of several Iraqi civilians, who either intentionally drove through TCPs or were caught in crossfires of combat operations, concerned CPA and other authorities. In response, BG Dempsey ordered a halt to the use of "snap" or "rolling" TCPs. Instead, all units reconfigured their TCPs to force vehicles to halt without the use of deadly force. One bright spot was the apparent reconstitution of the Iraqi police forces by the end of the summer. The police apprehended car thieves daily and made positive inroads against Baghdad crime. Counterfeiters were rounded up in August–September and provided information leading to more arrests. Most importantly, counterfeiting equipment was confiscated and removed from circulation. Other black marketeering continued, however, with serious problems created for fuel distribution and other aspects of daily life in Baghdad.

By the New Year, TF 1st Armored Division had overcome end-of-year fuel shortages, exacerbated by theft and black market trading, and the attacks on US soldiers had subsided. Partly, this situation resulted from the increased experience US troops had with enemy tactics, ambush patterns, and employment of IEDs. Soldiers and other observers detected the IEDs more readily, the growing Iraqi security forces provided better surveillance and acted with equal motivation against the IED employment, and the enemy mortar and rocket crews had withdrawn to firing positions at the extreme limit of range. The enemy remained flexible enough to introduce new tactical measures, however. Their use of mortars grew more frequent and a series of MANPADS launches against aircraft in the BIAP landing pattern demonstrated that their skill and imagination could not be underestimated.

Major operations

The soldiers settled into the demands of daily security operations and stabilization operations in Baghdad. In addition to these tasks, the division tried to tilt the balance against the various threats by launching specific tactical operations. The accomplishments of TF 1st Armored Division in these major operations form a significant part of its record in Iraq.

The division dubbed its first operation *Iron Dig* (June 2–11, 2003). This operation was intended to prove the death of Saddam Hussein by finding his remains in a bombed restaurant in Baghdad. Iraqi citizens, however, would not be reassured that Hussein was gone for several more months. Almost immediately a theater-wide operation began. Operation *Scorpion Sting* (June 15–29) intended to capture or kill significant numbers of FRL leaders thought to be responsible for the remainder of attacks on coalition forces.

As the heat of the summer set in, TF 1st Armored Division planned Operation *Iron Mountain* (July 14–18) to spoil expected attacks during the former regime holidays from July 14 to 17. New force protection measures protected the task force camps during these sensitive few days.

US soldiers mourned their dead in unit memorial formations. The typical soldier's memorial ceremony may be this one for a sergeant in 1/37th Armor, held in a FOB. The boots, rifle and helmet remain traditional markers of the fighting man. Two awards are placed one either side in this case: the Purple Heart medal and a valor award, such as the bronze star or army commendation medal. The field ceremony is both formal and informal, with a formation, honors, a senior officer eulogy, and a moment of silence.

Operation *Iron Bounty* (July 26–28) soon followed after information regarding Fedayeen militia surfaced. *Iron Bounty* resulted in the capture of several insurgents and intelligence details.

Operation *Longstreet* (August 26–September 9) was designed to stop insurgents operating in the border areas between divisions.

In these theater-wide operations, TF 1st Armored Division played a major role, particularly on its western border with the 82d Airborne Division. Several new projects also began around this time. The division began the construction of Kirzah (renamed Butler) Range and initiated the sometimes controversial mosque intelligence collection program. Task forces and engineers constructed various projects to improve the infrastructure of Baghdad. All of these programs lasted several months and were considered successful.

Soldier morale was taxed during this time because of extremely high temperatures, poor living conditions, continued fighting, and confirmation that the task force would be in Iraq for a full year. TF 1st Armored Division had several responses to the morale problems, starting with the mid-tour leave program. Additionally, the R&R program continued to send people to Qatar and the Green Zone. Living conditions were improved and morale slowly took an upswing.

The occupation force next faced the Ramadan holidays. Several restrictions, including curfew, were lifted from the Iraqi citizens to allow for a better holiday. Unfortunately, the task force experienced several attacks during the opening of Ramadan. The response was Operation *Iron Hammer* (November 12–27), an out-of-sector action in Karbala by elements of 2d Brigade, sent to quell an insurrection. This operation included air support, additional checkpoints, raids, and attacks. The display of force during Operation *Iron Hammer* suppressed the insurgents' Ramadan offensive. Shortly after the end of Ramadan, an operation was designed to disrupt the Iraqi black market. Operation *Iron Justice* (December 1–21) had a noticeably positive result on the weapons and fuel markets in Baghdad.

Shortly after Operation *Iron Justice*, troops of 4th Infantry Division captured Saddam Hussein near his hometown of Tikrit. Several operations followed the capture to exploit the intelligence from the former dictator. Operation *Iron Grip* (December 19, 2003–January 6, 2004) and Operation *Iron Resolve* (January 16–March 8) netted several FRL leaders and painted a much clearer picture of the former regime resistance in Iraq.

The planned turnover of occupation duties to the incoming 1st Cavalry Division began in February for some units. Operation *Iron Resolve* was designed to hold insurgents in check and show American resolve while the TOA took place. It was clear at this point that additional foreign and local elements had joined the insurgency. The most obvious new enemy included the local al-Qaeda group led by the acknowledged terrorist Abu-Musab al-Zarqawi.

As the division prepared to rotate back to its garrisons in Germany, a massive new rebellion started when the CPA shut down a newspaper of a young Shi'a cleric. Stability in southern Iraq and Sadr City (in Baghdad) quickly disintegrated. The Shi'a insurgency, combined with the major Marine Corps directed offensive in Fallujah, extended the stay of TF 1st Armored Division for an additional three months. The maneuver brigades from the task force spread across south-central Iraq to their new areas of operation. Brigades (some of which had already turned in ammunition and sent major equipment and troop contingents to Kuwait) changed their focus to high-intensity combat missions in the Shi'a strongholds of Karbala, al-Kut, Kufa, and an Najaf. In Operation *Iron Sabre* (April 16–July 7), soldiers took the fight to the insurgents. In July, the main body of the division began redeployment operations.

This three-month period provided the most extreme test of the mettle of 1st Armored Division, 2d ACR, and supporting and attached units. The redeployment to home station had already begun. Now, thoughts of home and family bitterly had to be set aside and the soldiers stood to as the division reorganized for the new fight. Of its total personnel strength of 23,655 soldiers, 1,820 had arrived already in Kuwait, and over 700 soldiers had returned to Germany as part of the advanced echelon elements under Operation *Iron Return*, and C Company, 1/6th Infantry had returned even earlier, because of its February 2003 deployment with V Corps. Between April 15 and May 13 724 soldiers returned from Germany to 1st Armored Division. These included such units as the Division Band, 75 soldiers from 2/501st Aviation and 115 soldiers of C/1/6th Infantry, the latter having begun reintegration under US Army, Europe (USAREUR) standards. Their equipment returned via shipping and the unit rejoined 2d Brigade in combat on May 5. The range of emotions experienced by these soldiers must be left to one's imagination.

After the battle

Operation *Iron Sabre* terminated on July 7, 2004, and the suspended Operation *Iron Return* resumed with a vengeance. Convoys again rolled to the south and the wash racks and docks now filled with the equipment of Old Ironsides. Because the bulk of the division lay south of Baghdad, most personnel flew out of Kuwait, just as they had arrived 15 months previously. By August all TF 1st Armored Division personnel had returned to Germany or the United States (2d ACR) except for some rear-party personnel still occupied with equipment retrograde.

On June 18 the division's official redeployment commenced when 159 soldiers returned to Germany, including 50 from the division headquarters. A week later all of the advanced echelons had redeployed and taken up their assignments. The division cased its colors on July 5 in Iraq and uncased them on July 14 at its headquarters in Wiesbaden. Most of the personnel redeployment took place during July 8–29, returning 99 percent of 1st Armored Division soldiers through the end of August. Every group of returning soldiers, regardless of how small, was met and welcomed at their posts by family readiness groups and community organizations. For many returning soldiers, this moment provided the first opportunity to "decompress"' from the constant dangers, tensions, and uncertainties of their "routine" lives as they had spent their last 15 months "downrange" (i.e. on the receiving end of fire).

The use of both Rhein Main (Frankfurt) and Ramstein air bases spread out the reception and aerial port clearance workload. The arrangements resulted in the arrival of the soldiers several weeks before the ships carrying their cargo docked. This measure facilitated the smooth introduction of both soldiers and equipment into the home station with sufficient time for soldiers to conduct "reintegration" activities before beginning the reconstitution of their equipment.

The commanding general of USAREUR prescribed *redeployment, reintegration, reconstitution,* and *retraining* in the form of orders and standards for the "4 Rs." These had emerged from experience gained by several deployments to the Balkans conducted in the 1990s.

Redeployment required synchronizing the movement of forces between Iraq or Kuwait and the posts in Germany. USAREUR established and operated appropriate control measures to effectively facilitate and manage the movement of units to and from Iraq/Kuwait. CENTCOM provided the same management for arrivals and departures in the theater of operations.

Reintegration was designed to ensure that redeploying soldiers reenergized their fighting spirit and nurtured their emotional and spiritual health and that of their families. It began prior to redeployment as units conducted reintegration tasks in Iraq in coordination with their rear detachments which initiated preparations at home stations. This 45-day reintegration process included attention to personal affairs, activities for single soldiers, and reuniting married soldiers with their families. These measures consisted in the main of as long a period of annual leave as could be afforded in each unit, while maintaining a shell of administrative presence, organized tours and recreational events, orientation and social services presentations and, if required, psychological and medical assistance to aid in the physical and emotional healing. It provided the opportunity for soldiers, civilians, and families to relax and learn how to live and work in their communities and become reacquainted with their friends and co-workers after a long and often stressful separation.

Reconstitution focused on rebuilding the combat power of units. The units reestablished combat service support relationships, and maintenance organizations focused their efforts on returning forces to ensure they were ready for worldwide contingencies. Reconstitution began before units left Iraq or Kuwait. Teams in Kuwait identified items requiring general support

The worst day for TF 1st Armored Division in Baghdad came with the death of eight soldiers in a single VBIED attack, producing this memorial ceremony in the FOB of 4/27th Field Artillery. An M109A6 self-propelled 155mm howitzer and M88A2 recovery vehicle remain parked in the background. On April 29, 2004 elements of 4/27th FA were escorting a TF Iron Claw engineer road sweep south of Baghdad. A station wagon approached the security element and stopped 50 meters short. When the soldiers approached it, the auto's payload of 200–400lb of explosives and mortar rounds detonated. Eight soldiers died and four were wounded and were evacuated immediately to a surgical hospital. The Iron Claw unit continued in its mission.

maintenance so they could be moved directly to appropriate facilities when they arrived in Europe. Other equipment returned to unit home stations for direct and organizational maintenance. The support provided by contractors also helped ensure that units were reconstituted effectively in a timely manner. This phase ended when units achieved materiel readiness standards commensurate with their authorized level of organization.

Retraining was initiated at home stations by conducting individual and collective retraining under the guidance established by the commander of the 7th Army Training Command in Germany. At the completion of home station training, units conducted gunnery training at the Grafenwöhr and Baumholder training areas and then held key training events to be certified as ready for operational missions.

For the 1st Armored Division, reintegration had already begun and an unsettling factor loomed when the Extension Campaign was announced and MG Dempsey informed the rear detachment commanders that the division would likely remain in Iraq for another 90–120 days. The USAREUR home front faced its greatest challenge as the initial shock of the news faded and its implications sank in. Letters in the *Stars and Stripes* newspaper over the two to three weeks after the announcement indicated that some family members felt betrayed and abandoned. Actions by the rear detachment support staffs and the timely appearance by BG Mark Hertling in the communities contributed much to the allaying of fears and disappointments among the families of Old Ironsides. The assistant division commander flew back to Germany and met with spouses during town meetings held on Friday, April 16 and Monday, April 19, 2004, in the military communities. At these meetings he shared his personal knowledge of the extension and what the soldiers were doing in Iraq, and attempted to allay concerns about their living conditions and specific situations. He was accompanied by the commanding general's wife, Mrs. Deanie Dempsey, and the 104th Area Support Group commander, who described the available community services and actions his command had taken. These interactions proved crucial because members of the community believed the Army representatives and felt that they shared an empathy with them. With the additional bonding brought by the Extension Campaign, the families and soldiers responded very positively to the final reintegration program. The large-scale granting of leave and the assistance afforded by the various community support agencies facilitated a moving and restoring period of time.

Retraining the division came last in the sequence, but its planning took place concurrently with reconstitution. During the period of October–December 2004 the focus remained on completion of reconstitution. But the division commander sought to use the early months of 2005 as an opportunity to retrain in warfighting skills, building on the wealth of experience gained in over 15 months of Operation *Iraqi Freedom*.

On October 12, 2004, MG Dempsey set his priorities:

We spent 1st Quarter for the most part in the garrison environment focusing on reconstitution of equipment, soldiers, and families. We will spend 2d Quarter for the most part in a field environment regaining our field craft and collective warfighting skills. At the individual and crew level, we must reestablish our credentials in marksmanship and gunnery. We are, after all, America's Tank Division, and should be expected to be the best in the world at putting steel on target. The collective training focus this quarter will be on squads and platoons culminating before the end of the quarter with squad and platoon external evaluations. Iron combat support [CS] and combat service support [CSS] soldiers will continue to focus on Sergeant's Time Training, and they will begin training on [gunnery] Tables VI through XII. This is a dramatic and important shift in the way we train our CS and CSS Soldiers. CMTC [Combat Maneuver Training Center, Hohenfels] rotations 05-04 and 05-05 as well as Iron Thunder 05-01 will be our opportunity to train both for potential HIC [high-intensity combat] and COIN [counterinsurgency] missions. This quarter is our best opportunity to show junior leaders what "right" looks like in training. We must reinforce the training management process and the eight-step training model. We must measure ourselves against doctrine and established task-condition-standards. We must train as a combined arms team. We <u>know</u> that we will deploy again in support of the Global War on Terror. This quarter and the next we must prepare our soldiers for combat. That is our sacred obligation.

From mid-April to early June, 1st and 2d brigades conducted both Level 1 gunnery, CMTC live fires, and maneuvers. At the same time, DIVARTY, Division Engineer, and DISCOM executed their Iron Warrior (individual weapons) firing tables. On June 21, 2005, Old Ironsides reported "combat ready" to V Corps and its soldiers stood retrained and prepared to answer the country's call.

MUSEUMS AND COLLECTIONS

The major government collections containing fighting vehicles, equipment, and uniforms used by the army in Baghdad remain the garrisons of the active forces (where usually a current vehicle type will be on display), museums of the divisions and separate regiments, as well as the training centers of the various branches. See, for example:

1st Armored Division Museum, Baumholder, Germany (soon moving to Ft. Bliss TX) http://www.1ad.army.mil/Museum/a_Museum.htm
Patton Museum, Ft. Knox
http://www.armorfortheages.com/
National Infantry Museum, Ft. Benning
http://www.benningmwr.com/museum.cfm
Artillery Museum, Ft. Sill
http://sill-www.army.mil/Museum/HOME%20PAGE.htm
Engineer Museum Ft. Leonard Wood
http://www.wood.army.mil/MUSEUM/

A few museums have acquired examples of current soldier apparel and personal gear, and reenactment groups of course do not exist, for action continues in Baghdad every day.

GLOSSARY

ACR	Armored Cavalry Regiment
ALICE	All-purpose Lightweight Individual Carrying Equipment
BCT	Brigade Combat Team
BDU	Battle Dress Uniform
BFV	Bradley Fighting Vehicle
BIAP	Baghdad International Airport
CERP	Commander's Emergency Response Program
CJTF	Commander Joint Task Force
CMTC	Combat Maneuver Training Center, Hohenfels Germany
CPA	Coalition Provisional Authority
CS and CSS	Combat Support and Combat Service Support
DCT	Division Artillery Combat Team, a regiment-sized headquarters controlling several artillery or other type battalions in support of division operations
DISCOM	Division Support Command, a regiment-sized headquarters controlling several service support or logistics battalions in support of division operations
DIVARTY	Division Artillery, a regiment-sized headquarters controlling several artillery battalions in support of division operations
DS	Direct Support
DoD	Department of Defense
FOB	Forward Operating Base
FPS	Facility Protection Services
FRL	Former Regime Loyalists
HMMWV	High Mobility Multipurpose Wheeled Vehicle; "Humvee" or "Hummer"
ICDC	Iraqi Civil Defense Corps, precursor to the NIA
IED	Improvised Explosive Device; formerly called "booby trap"
MANPADS	Man-Portable Air Defense Systems; hand-held antiaircraft missiles
MOS	Military Occupational Specialty
MP	Military Police
NIA	New Iraqi Army
NCO	Non-Commissioned Officer, i.e. corporal and above
OTV	Outer Tactical Vest (of Interceptor body armor system)
PASGT	Personnel Armor System Ground Troops
REDCON	Readiness Condition
RPG	(Ruchnoy Protivotankoviy Granatomet) or "handheld antitank projectile launcher;" erroneously referred to as "rocket propelled grenade" by media and pundits; derived from RPG family of weapons originally fielded by the USSR
SAPI	Small Arms Protective Inserts
SAW	Squad Automatic Weapon
SCIRI	Supreme Council for the Islamic Revolution in Iraq; a Shi'ite political party and armed militia
SOSO	Stability Operations and Support Operations
SPOD	Sea Port of Departure
TCP	Traffic Control Point
TF	Task Force
TOA	Transfer of Authority
UAH	Up-Armored HMMWV
USAREUR	United States Army, Europe
USCENTCOM	United States Central Command, the combatant command assigned to the area roughly east of Israel and west of India, and from Kazakhstan south to Kenya
UXO	Unexploded Ordnance

In the final analysis, the mission of 1st Armored Division's task force in Baghdad was to protect the Iraqi population. Here soldiers of 2d Brigade, 82d Airborne present information at a local school to inform the children of the dangers of unexploded and stray ordnance materiel that remained all too common in the neighborhoods.

BIBLIOGRAPHY

Atkinson, Rick, *In The Company of Soldiers: A Chronicle of Combat in Iraq*, New York: Henry Holt and Co. (2004)

Beck, Sara, and Malcolm Downing, *The Battle for Iraq: BBC News Correspondents on the War Against Saddam*, Baltimore: Johns Hopkins Press (2003)

Fontenoy, Gregory, E. J. Degen, and David Tohn, *On Point: The United States Army in Operation* Iraqi Freedom, Fort Leavenworth: Combat Studies Institute Press (2004)

Gordon, Michael R., and Bernard E. Trainor, *Cobra II: The Inside Story of the Invasion and Occupation of Iraq*, New York: Pantheon (2006)

Granger, Martha G., "The 1st AD in Operation *Iraqi Freedom,*" *Military Review* (November–December 2004), pp.7–11

Kuester, Sean, "Using the Patrol Brief in Baghdad," *Armor* (July–August 2004), pp.29–33

Murray, Dale, Gregory Hickerson, Michael Gantert, David Tosh, and Morris Estep, "Company-Level Cordon and Search Operations in Iraq," "Methods for IED Reconnaissance and Detection," "Checkpoint and Traffic Control Point Operations," "Engaging the Population and Local Leaders," "Integrating Local Security Forces during Combat and Stability Operations," *Armor* (September–October 2004), pp.26–47

Record, Jeffrey, *Dark Victory: America's Second War against Iraq*, Annapolis: Naval Institute Press (2004)

Reynolds, Nicholas E., *Basrah, Baghdad and Beyond: The US Marine Corps in the Second Iraq War*, Annapolis: Naval Institute Press (2005)

van Creveld, Martin, *The Transformation of War*, New York: Free Press (1991)

White, [Robert] Pat[rick], "Task Force Iron Dukes Campaign for Najaf," *Armor* (November–December 2004), pp.7–12

Web sites

http://jccc.afis.osd.mil/images/images.pl?Lbox= defenselink.Operation_IRAQI_FREEDOM&tc =12&cc=3&vn=1&show_vn=on&ban

http://www.operations.mod.uk/telic/photo_ gallery.htm

http://www.defence.gov.au/opfalconer/ gallery.htm

http://www.au.af.mil/au/awc/awcgate/crs/ rs21578.pdf

http://www.abc.net.au/4corners/stories/ s695368.htm

The final garrison posture at the end of TF 1st Armored Division's campaign in Baghdad consisted of the eight Expeditionary FOBs built for the 1st Cavalry Division to occupy as it relieved 1st Armored Division. Outlined in green, they dominated the Green Zone, but otherwise removed most US forces to the city perimeter. Note: DIVARTY had replaced 2d/82d in South Baghdad at this point.

Although most artillery of TF 1st Armored Division remained out of use, with the battery personnel deployed as infantrymen, the 4.2-in. mortars of the task force provided most of the indirect fire support, especially when an accurate and timely plot of insurgent firing positions could be made. Here an M106A2 mortar carrier of 1st Brigade fires at night.

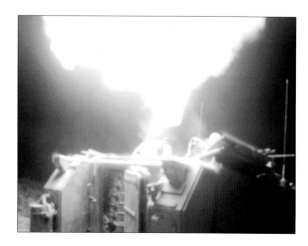

COLOR PLATE COMMENTARY

A: US INFANTRYMEN 1ST BATTALION, 36TH INFANTRY "SPARTANS," 2004

These soldiers wear the typical clothing and equipment worn while serving in the Baghdad security and stability mission. One wears the desert three-color camouflage BDU, without equipment (**1**). It consists of hat, shirt, and trousers worn over a light brown t-shirt and underwear, with a black web belt. The shirt has breast and lower pockets with flaps, while the trousers contain four standard type pockets, two leg-bellows type pockets, and reinforcement patches added at the knees and buttocks. The desert boot is cut from soft leather for natural venting, without the venting holes that admit sand in other models. The BDU cap comes in several models for warm or cold temperatures. Note the US Army patch and name patch over left and right breast pockets. Above the name patch are the special qualification badges, in this case the combat infantryman insignia over the master parachutist badge.

The second figure (**2**) wears "full battle rattle" – the BDU uniform, helmet, Interceptor body armor (green camo) without collar or other attachments, ballistic goggles, AN/PVS mount on helmet, M4 carbine with sights, 4× scope, infrared pointer, and 40mm grenade launcher (note web sling of weapon around neck). Crossing over the left shoulder is the water tube from Camelbak® water carrier. The armored vest carries magazine and grenade pouches, bayonet/sheath, and Motorola Talk About radio.

The other illustrations show: PASGT Helmet with an AN/PVS-14 scope (**3**), Body Armor, Interceptor (**4**), Camelbak® Classic Hydration Pack (**5**), M9 pistol with holster (**6**), M4 carbine, with scope, pointer and grenade launcher, 30-round magazine (**7**), Magazine pouches (**8**), goggles – close-quarter combat (**9**) and service issue sand & sun (**10**) types, boots (**11**), compass & first aid carrier (**12**), knee pads (**13**), M9 bayonet with scabbard (**14**), and bush hat (**15**).

B: CLOSE-QUARTERS BATTLE DRILL, 2D BATTALION, 325TH AIRBORNE INFANTRY "WHITE FALCONS"

Four soldiers – arranged in the "short stack" for urban combat – practice movements before going on a raid. The minimum full battle gear includes rifle/SAW, body armor, helmet, ammo pouches, plus any combination of gloves, pads, eyewear, knives, and pistols. One carries the M249 SAW. Navigating down hallways and securing rooms, the soldiers will yell out their positions to each other. Each man has an assigned task. The team spreads down the walls until all corners have been locked down and secured. The house they've just secured is two-dimensional. Its walls are strips of white engineer tape pinned into the ground in assorted rectangular shapes. This "dwelling" is known as a "Glass House." The house may be a life-size floor plan, but the action inside is just as real to the soldiers as if it were somebody's home. "The first house that we came into in Iraq – we were so surprised at the layout," said SSG Rogelio Cortes, 2d Platoon squad leader, C Company, 1st Battalion, 36th Infantry. "It was a lesson learned. After we did our first house raid, we had to adjust how we thought it would look."

C: PROTECTING THE TROOPS, 2003–04

Pictured here are some cargo/personnel variants of the HMMWV series and not the weapons and missile carrier vehicles that were manufactured with "basic" and "supplemental" armor. These carriers also received similar upgrades as the threat increased and new materials became available.

1. Improvised Armor: protected with scrap plate, armored glass, and Kevlar® sections "scrounged" from dumps and damaged vehicles.
2. Up-Armored HMMWV: The UAH weighs about 2,000lb (909kg) more than the standard HMMWV and includes

1st Armored Division soldiers train in a "shooting house" where live-fire engagements are practiced against target dummies set up in simulated situations of house-to-house fighting or surprise engagements. Non-combatant (i.e. civilian) persons are also represented in the target array, so that soldiers must distinguish targets in the exercise.

200lb (91kg) steel-plated doors, steel plating under the cab and several layers of bonded, ballistic-resistant glass to replace zip-up plastic windows.

3. Armor Survivability Kit (ASK): The kit weighs half of that designed for the UAH, providing some RPG and IED protection.

4. HMMWV Armored Demountable (HArD) Kit: This kit is an industry development providing interchangeable armor components for most HMMWV variants. It includes side, roof, and underbody armoring at a high level of ballistic and blast protection. "Sub-kits" provide only the armor protection desired, to retain a better vehicle payload.

Two body armor systems are displayed:

5. The Personnel Armor System Ground Troops Vest (PASGT-V) replaced the old "flak jacket" models worn during the Korean and Vietnam wars. The ballistic protection of 13 plies of aramid Kevlar® 29 fabric is woven under the shell of ballistic nylon cloth, with woodland camouflage exterior reversible to olive green. The vest has a removable three-quarter collar, pivoting shoulder pads, two front pockets, and two grenade hangers. It provides superior protection against fragmentation impacts, but will not resist rifle-caliber shots at close distance.

6. The Interceptor Multi-Threat Body Armor System consists of two components: the OTV, and SAPI plates (**7**). It combines the best characteristics of the older and newer vests by the ballistic protection the vest offers against fragments and pistol-caliber bullets, with the option of adding the heavier front and back plates (with side and shoulder protection procured later – "deltoid auxiliary protectors") to defend against rifle-caliber (7.62mm) bullets.

The tandem issues of body armor and armor kits for utility vehicles became pressing in both military and political arenas once combat continued in 2003 after the "end of major combat operations," when the Iraqi insurgency gained momentum. There seems no doubt that military requirements for the armoring of utility vehicles never intended for use in close combat came as a surprise to the logistics system, and the response proved predictably belated as casualties grew. Likewise, the provision of the new Interceptor armor system to the troops was only partial at the time of the 2003 invasion, and priorities of issue certainly left large numbers of them with the older pattern of PASGT armor vests. Moreover, defective quality control and the delays in providing upgrades to Interceptor components (heavier SAPI, additional side and shoulder protection) exacerbated the political uproar. Although much publicity came from the political opposition to the war, there seems little doubt that the American government and forces underestimated the scope and ferocity of the occupation struggle. The response of the military laboratories has been to design almost total protection for vehicles and persons alike, but like the metal-armored knights of the late Middle Ages, the future use of the proposed systems may result in the troops discarding or omitting to use many such components, as is already in evidence in Iraq today.

D: US INFANTRY OF 2D BATTALION, 6TH INFANTRY "GATORS" ON RAID

Targeting a bombmaker's hideaway revealed by intelligence services, troops of the 2d Brigade, 1st Armored Division close in to isolate and assault the suspect building. The minimum full battle gear for such combat operations worn by the troops consists of rifle/SAW, body armor, helmet, ammo and grenade pouches, plus an array of gloves, pads, eyewear, knives, pistols, and so forth. From a dismount position, the troops leave their vehicles and move rapidly to take the center building from the right flank. An additional section watches the building on the left.

The raids typically result from tip-offs made by Iraqis increasingly willing to inform Americans about the groups attacking them, and this early morning raid was the result of one such tip. "I think what we found at the building helped to confirm information that we had, and gave us new indications of future, planned activities that we'll look into," said LTC T. C. Williams, 2/6th Infantry's commander. "We took a good chunk out of the guys responsible for the majority of enemy activity."

The Gators carefully planned the operation to capture the targets simultaneously and take full advantage of the element of surprise. The raid went off without a hitch. "Every one of these missions that's quiet is a good one," Williams said. "You go in with plenty of combat power, which certainly discourages the 'bad guys' from doing anything." Part of the search included dog handlers from a civilian K-9 contractor, who brought their explosive-detecting canine partners to various raid sites to sniff out bomb-making materials. The raid did not net all the fish the Gators were trying to catch, Williams said; but the battalion did hook nine suspects: six of the targeted individuals, plus three others who tested positive for having been involved with explosives. "Now [having more insurgents off the streets] gives us the opportunity to do projects in a more secure environment," said Williams.

E: A FORWARD OPERATING BASE (FOB), BAGHDAD, NOVEMBER 2003

Daily life in an FOB encompassed the various housekeeping needs of the troops, plus some amount of recreation. The workload centered around maintenance of equipment, guard duty, and preparing for operations outside the FOB: patrols, checkpoints, convoys, raids, and searches for the most part. Apart from training needs, the uniform and equipment requirements were relaxed and there was a possibility of a moment of relaxation to read and write letters, make a telephone call, or hang out with friends. The FOBs came in various sizes, especially in the early days, when so many Iraqi military sites, palaces, and industrial sites became available. Later, these were turned over to Iraqi government use or became patrol bases. The 26 second-generation FOBs ready in the fall of 2003 contained the amenities for troop life necessary to sustain morale during the year's deployment. The third-generation camps, Expeditionary Camps, came on line in the spring of 2004, are designed to last ten years, and hold up to 12,000 troops.

Each camp has a defensive perimeter, usually based upon a wall and ditch combination, watched over by guard towers. There are also mobile or roving patrols around larger FOBs and a reaction force stands ready in case of intrusions or other threats. The gates are especially fortified and even fitted with metal detector systems to permit rapid searches of the large numbers of Iraqi workers employed for services and construction in the FOB.

F: COMBAT AT KARBALA, TF 1ST BATTALION, 37TH ARMOR "BANDITS," MAY 2004

Under the protection and fire of a tank and BFV, dismounted infantrymen work along the far side of the street, in what had been a busy, prosperous neighborhood of the city. They are looking into or briefly entering the storefronts, but several men remain oriented toward the more distant buildings, watching for snipers or other enemies. The tank fires its cannon at the right rear building to eliminate a sniper position.

The M1A1 Abrams tank and M2A2 BFV are the mainstays of US armored and mechanized infantry divisions. The tank has older NATO woodland camouflage, long faded by a year in Iraq, covered with the sand and dust of the environment. The M2A2 has been repainted to desert scheme. The Abrams' 120mm cannon proved highly useful in urban fighting. Its accuracy and the excellent fuzing of the explosive ammunition meant it could be used against specific targets without running the risk of ricochets or excessive penetration of solid bullets into adjoining buildings or neighborhoods, as could happen with the 25mm chain gun of the Bradley or the .50-cal. tank commander's weapon.

TF 1/37th Armor took its tank and mechanized infantry companies into action in Karbala in the final major action of Operation *Iron Sabre*, the suppression of the al-Sadr rising in April–July 2004. Several hundred enemy fighters roamed at

will over the city, except for around the two coalition FOBs on the outskirts. Upon its arrival in early May, the battalion task force established a cordon and search of the vital al-Mukhayem mosque and began to secure the surrounding neighborhood. Fighting house to house, the Bandits not only rescued Iraqi police officers, but also liberated the civilians trapped in their homes by the al-Sadr militia threats. By May 21, the tide had shifted and civil affairs operations could be mounted and the city restored to normalcy. The final action by Old Ironsides was to establish a weapons buy back program. In the course of about a week, it paid out nearly $1 million in $200 increments for weapons and ammunition.

G: US TANK CREWMAN, 2D BATTALION, 70TH ARMOR "THUNDERBOLT," 2004

This soldier (1), shown in the tank commander's position of the M1A1 tank, wears the regulation nomex crewman uniform in olive green, with the 1st Armored Division patch on the shoulder, US Army patch over left breast pocket, and name over right breast pocket; and the CVC helmet with black external shell.

The tankers in Baghdad and other areas frequently had to dismount and act or assist other troops in apprehending street criminals or insurgents, and even executed impromptu raids using several crewmen from the same platoon. In those cases, they discarded the nomex flame-resistant tanker suit (it also retained heat worse than the standard uniform) and equipped themselves in a similar manner to the infantrymen. Although armored fighting vehicle crews took their turns with all other soldiers of TF 1st Armored Division in guard duty and dismounted raids and patrols, they retained at all times their combat orientation and capabilities as crewmen, assisted by continuous training and proficiency. The payoff came in Operation *Iron Sabre*, when conventional combat ensued between US forces and Mahdi militiamen loyal to Muqtada al-Sadr.

Also depicted are the following typical items worn or at hand in combat:

2. goggles, sand & sun
3. helmet, CVC. It is exploded to show exterior shell (**3a**) colors usually black, green, or sand, H4 interior communication and padding harness (**3b**), headphones with boom microphone (**3c**)
4. M9 pistol, shoulder holster
5. Nomex gloves
6. M4 carbine and magazines
7. body armor, PASGT and Interceptor
8. tanker boots, a personal purchase item

This soldier takes advantage of some off-duty time at his FOB to head for the swimming pool. By the fall of 2003, most of the FOBs, although still of the "temporary" type, had been rebuilt, with living and recreational amenities required to keep soldiers in a sustainable state of morale for their unending occupation duties. In addition to providing a secure environment, the FOBs afforded a measure of relaxation, internet contact with home and the outside world, access to service stores and fitness centers, plus sound and video entertainment commensurate with their lives in home stations. Thus, the FOB system served simultaneously the tactical and administrative systems of the US forces.

INDEX

References to illustrations are shown in **bold**. Plates are shown with page and caption locators in brackets